CW00746736

NARROW GAUGE RAILWAYS OF TAIWAN

Sugar, Shays and Toil

Michael Reilly

Published by Mainline & Maritime Ltd
3 Broadleaze, Upper Seagry, near Chippenham, Wiltshire, SN15 5EY
www.mainlineandmaritime.co.uk
orders@mainlineandmaritime.co.uk
01275 845012

ISBN: 978-1-900340-46-5

© Mainline & Maritime Ltd and the Author 2017
All rights reserved.
No part of this publication may be reproduced by any process
without the prior written permission of the publisher.

All uncredited photographs taken by the Author.

Designed and typeset by Mach 3 Solutions Ltd (www.mach3solutions.co.uk)
Printed in the UK

Cover picture captions:
Front: A centenarian at work: Shay no 31 (Lima 2946 of 1917) of the Alishan Forestry Railway outside the shed at Alishan, 27 September 2017.
Title: TSC no 370 (Tubize 2354 of 1948), heads a tourist train through the countryside near Wushulin mill, 16 February 2008.
Back: The year is 1972 and the afternoon mixed from Tuchang to Lotung crosses one of the extensive trestles on the Lotung Forestry Railway behind loco no 5. *Kurashige Nobutaka*

CONTENTS

LIST OF MAPS

Apart from the historical map of the Taiwanese railway system in the 1930s, the maps were drawn by John Athersuch. The overview maps were based on information from a variety of sources, including Charles Small's 'Rails to the Setting Sun' and 'Rails to the Mines,' and Plato Chen (陳勤忠) in respect of the mine railways in the Pingxi valley. The individual maps of the logging railways are based on the first full cartographic survey of Taiwan, undertaken by the Land Survey Department of the General Staff Headquarters of the Japanese Imperial Army between approximately 1910 and 1925. This remained the only comprehensive survey of Taiwan until quite recently, later maps produced by both the US military and the USSR being based almost entirely on it. A nearly complete set of the 1:50,000 scale maps produced from this survey is accessible online from Stanford University at https://library.stanford.edu/guides/gaihozu-japanese-imperial-maps.

Almost the whole of the Taipingshan system (and indeed the east coast logging railways) post-dated the survey so does not appear on maps. In this case the route of the lines was taken from Forestry Bureau maps then super-imposed on the original Japanese ones. The sketch plan of the layout at Jhulin station is taken from 太平山開發史 *(Taipingshan Kaifanshi – History of Taipingshan Development) by Lin Qing chi (林清池).*

ACKNOWLEDGEMENTS

This book would never have been written without the support, encouragement and help of many friends in Taiwan, above all members of Taiwan's Railway Culture Society, in particular Wente Lo (羅文德), Nai-yi Hsu (許乃懿), Min-chang Cheng (鄭銘彰) and Tzai-Der Wang (王在德), who did so much to introduce me to the charms of the country's sugar mill railways and much more of its railways generally. Their enthusiasm was infectious, their hospitality and encouragement knew no bounds. Taiwan's professional railwaymen were also extremely supportive and helpful, none more so than Hung-Kang Sung (宋鴻康) of the Bureau of High Speed Rail in the Ministry of Transport and Jhy-Ping Lin (林治平) of the Alishan Forest Railway, to whom I am especially grateful for access to the inner sanctum of the line's operations at Chiayi and its engineering marvel at Dulishan, as well as much more of the railway.

Jennie Lin provided invaluable pointers and help on the ground for initial research on the line at Pahsienshan, by some measure the least well known and researched of all the lines covered. She also introduced me to Plato Chen (陳勤忠), whose knowledge of the history of the Pingxi valley mines is rivalled only by his own enthusiasm for the subject and who did so much to advance my own limited knowledge of their railway lines. The push-cart lines of Taiwan are a fascinating but little known subject, especially given their social and economic impact on the country. Without the advice and guidance of Chen Chia-hao (陳家豪) of the Institute of Taiwan History at Academia Sinica, this chapter of the book would have been a blank. Other colleagues at Academia Sinica, most especially Michael Hsiao (蕭新煌), were more than generous with their time and in offering advice and suggestions, while Teresa Yu (游德怡) was equally generous with all-important administrative support.

In Japan, Ichiro Junpu generously acted as a source of general advice and liaison as well as supplying me with a copy of the Kato Works builder's list while Noriyuki Natori provided me with that for Nippon Sharyo, both essential for gaining a deeper knowledge of the motive power on many of the lines.

The book would have been poor indeed without the many historic and atmospheric photographs. I am indebted to Masaaki Umemura, Nicholas Pertwee, Kurashige Nobutaka, Su Chao Hsu and Robin Gibbons for the use of theirs or ones from their collections and to Rob Dickinson for those of the late John Tillman. Marc Plumb's *taipics.com* proved a most useful source of older pictures.

I owe at least as big a debt to John Raby and John Athersuch, both of whom kindly read an early version of the text and made many helpful suggestions for improvements. The former also contributed photographs and information from his own time in Taiwan, especially on the last days of the Pingxi valley lines and put me in touch with others who also contributed, while the latter gave very generously of his time to prepare the excellent maps which add considerably to the information given in the text. Richard Faulkner very kindly agreed to provide the Foreword and has been more than generous with his comments therein.

Librarians at Academia Sinica and in Taiwan's National Central Library were unfailingly patient and helpful in dealing with my requests, however esoteric or arcane they may have been. Finally, but by no means least, I owe a big debt to the Ministry of Foreign Affairs in Taiwan for the generous grant of a Taiwan Fellowship. While this was primarily for research in areas not related to railways, it also gave an unmissable opportunity to undertake further, more thorough research especially in archival sources, as well as to visit or revisit many of the railways or sites covered. The result is a more informed, more detailed and more accurate book than would otherwise have been possible. I am most grateful to all. The errors that remain in the text are entirely and solely my responsibility.

While popular, especially at weekends, the cost of maintaining mills and railways as tourist attractions has perhaps proved greater than initially expected. By 2016 the trains at Suantou mill were looking distinctly careworn. 29 May 2016.

FOREWORD

by
Lord Faulkner of Worcester

Railways will remain safe in the midst of panic; and though times of pressure, severe, hazardous, ruinous pressure, have been felt in this country, and unfortunately must be felt again, yet it will only prove them to be part and parcel of the genuine sources of wealth and avenues for labour, in which this country lives and moves and has its being.

These words were written in 1851 by someone called John Francis in his book *A History of the English Railway*. Substitute "Taiwanese" for "English", fast forward 60 years, and we can begin to understand how important the building of railways was for the creation of Taiwan as a modern industrialised society, noting in passing that there's been no shortage of pressure which has had to be overcome along the way.

Those thirsty for knowledge about how this came about have had few written resources on which to draw, but this deficiency has now been redressed by Michael Reilly in this wonderful history of the narrow gauge railways of Taiwan, and I am honoured and delighted to have been asked by him to write the foreword to it.

It is not unusual for distinguished British diplomats to maintain a soft spot for the countries where they have served, and for them to return there, often on holiday, after their careers have moved them on to new postings or into retirement.

Michael has done more than that. He came back to Taiwan, took up an academic fellowship awarded by the Taiwanese government, and has written this definitive and authoritative history about a unique aspect of life there.

This book will be appreciated by a wide variety of audiences. The railway enthusiasts will not be able to put it down. They will find fascinating his account of how an extraordinary variety of railways of different narrow gauges played critical roles in the exploiting and developing of Taiwan's forestry, sugar refining, coal mining, salt extraction and later, tourist industries. They will marvel at the skill of the railway builders in overcoming the most enormous engineering obstacles round, through and across the highest mountains in the region. And they will enjoy reading about the procurement and operation of locomotives and rolling stock from different countries, and about the extraordinary story of the 3,000km of push-cart railways – hand-powered tramways – built to a gauge of slightly less than half a metre.

Students of political and social history will find much to interest them too. It was a colonial power – Japan – that was responsible for the construction, equipping and operation of Taiwan's railways for 50 years, and their legacy is very much with us today, particularly in respect of station buildings, and the ancient coaches and locomotives found on display in museum settings.

There is a third group of people who will thank Michael for producing this book – those who are thinking of visiting Taiwan as tourists but haven't yet done so. If they have any interest in railways – modern, as well as ancient – they will find few places in the Far East more welcoming and with so much to see.

I commend this scholarly yet immensely readable book unreservedly.

Richard Faulkner is president of the Heritage Railway Association and the British Prime Minister's trade envoy to Taiwan. He has served in the House of Lords since 1999, and is the co-author of two acclaimed political and social histories of Britain's railways in the second half of the 20th century.

TSC no 370 (Tubize 2354 of 1948) with its auxiliary water tank is seen in action at Annei sugar mill, near Chiayi.

Nicholas Pertwee

INTRODUCTION

My interest in narrow gauge railways goes back to childhood. A very welcome Christmas present as a young boy was a copy of Pat Whitehouse and Peter Allen's *Round the World on the Narrow Gauge.* Published in 1966, it sought to encapsulate what was already by then a vanishing era. I quickly came to regard it as a bible, spending many hours both then and since poring over its photographs. I still have it on my bookshelves and it has long outlasted most Christmas presents.

But it was very much a book of its time. Reflecting the geo-politics of the 1960s, China got just one sentence. Taiwan merited two:

> *…there are two narrow gauge lines of 3ft 6in and 2ft 6in. gauge, memorials to the Japanese occupation after the War of 1895. We pass them by for the best of reasons.*

By the mid-1970s although diesels had largely taken over main line working on the Alishan Forestry Railway, Shays were still a common sight on shunting duties at Alishan and logging work in the mountains. Two-cylinder Shay no 18 of the Alishan Forestry Railway (Lima works no 2632 of 1918) prepares a loaded log train at Alishan in this September 1974 photograph. No 18 was one of the last five Shays to remain in service, lasting until the formal end of steam working on the line on 1 November 1984. It is now on display in the old running shed at Fenchihu station.

John Tillman

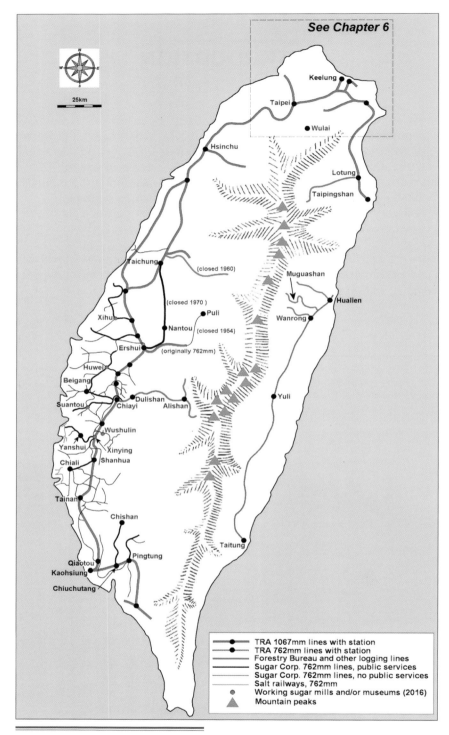

25km

Keelung

Taipei

Wulai

Hsinchu

Lotung

Taipingshan

Taichung

(closed 1960)

Muguashan

(closed 1970)

Xihu   Puli

Nantou   (closed 1954)

Hualien

Wanrong

Ershui

(originally 762mm)

Huwei

Beigang

Suantou   Dulishan

Chiayi   Alishan

Yuli

Wushulin

Yanshui   Xinying

Chiali   Shanhua

Tainan

Chishan

Taitung

Qiaotou   Pingtung

Kaohsiung

Chiuchutang

●━━●	TRA 1067mm lines with station
●──●	TRA 762mm lines with station
	Forestry Bureau and other logging lines
	Sugar Corp. 762mm lines, public services
	Sugar Corp. 762mm lines, no public services
	Salt railways, 762mm
●	Working sugar mills and/or museums (2016)
▲	Mountain peaks

Taiwan's railway network in 1970: Taiwan's phenomenal economic growth was just getting under way and apart from the disappearance of most push-cart lines (not shown here) the railway network remained little changed from fifty years earlier.

John Athersuch

Narrow gauge territory, Taiwan style (1). Improbable though it may seem, a busy narrow gauge line once ran through here. The buildings on the left of the photo are on the site of an aerial ropeway platform. From here a line ran for some 4km passing immediately beneath where the photo was taken and hugging the contours to another ropeway station which gave access to a further line higher up the mountain. From there, the system fanned out to create a network of 100km at peak extent, almost all of it 1000 metres or more above sea level. Taipingshan, 25 September 2016.

It was accurate in so far as it went and no doubt in common with most readers, I took the somewhat Delphic second sentence to mean that there was no working steam left – this was 1966 after all, and steam was already in retreat around the world. Another decade was to pass before I learnt that, like a Ministerial answer to a Parliamentary Question, while technically correct it was far from being the whole story. There was more, much more, to Taiwan's railways than this brief dismissal, including some fascinating Shays in the mountains. Only when I finally paid my first visit to the island in 1983 did I realise just how big an understatement and how inaccurate it was. There was, and still is, a '3ft 6in line.' This is the network of the state-owned Taiwan Railways Administration (TRA) which in 1966 was over 800km in extent and an enthusiast's heaven, with steam locomotives out-numbering diesels on its roster and well over 50% of trains still steam hauled. The TRA also owned a '2ft 6in gauge' line, isolated from the rest of the system and running for 170km along the rift valley in the island's remote south east. But this was no narrow gauge line in the conventional

Opposite: This satellite map from NASA clearly shows the challenges facing the railway builder in Taiwan: the high mountains extend almost the entire length of the island and are split by deep valleys subject to frequent landslides. Agriculture, industry and population are all concentrated in the western plains. Earthquakes add further to the civil engineering challenge.

NASA

light railway sense. True, the route included several switchbacks or zigzags, indicative of steep gradients and low-cost construction, and in 1966 the bulk of freight traffic was hauled by slow moving 0-8-0 tank locomotives. But interspersed with the freight were express railcars running at speeds of up to 70km/h and more remarkable still, a nightly sleeping car service, by then surely unique on the 762mm gauge.

But the government system was only a part – and not even the major one – of an extensive network of narrow gauge lines throughout the country. In probably no other country in the world did narrow gauge railways play such a major role in national development as they did in Taiwan. Built to bring sugar cane from the fields, timber from the mountains, coal from mines and salt from the flats, at its peak Taiwan's sub-3ft 6in railway network was almost 4000km in extent, or five times the length of the country's principal railway system. This was remarkable enough. More so was that nearly 1300km of this was hand-powered tramways or 'push-cart lines' on 495mm gauge or thereabouts. The concept had been developed by Decauville in France but was to see greater take up, and last far longer, in Taiwan than in his home country. Some of the lines were also to develop a level of sophistication probably unimagined by Decauville, extending to 30km in length or even more, sometimes with occasional tunnels and even double track running. But the variety did not end there. More conventional motive power came from suppliers on three continents and spanning the alphabet from Alco to Vulcan, while fuel sources included charcoal gas, petrol and ethanol as well as coal, diesel oil and very occasionally electric power.

Maybe most remarkable of all was how long it lasted. Push-cart lines were almost – but not quite – history by the mid-1960s but on that first 1983 visit steam could still be found on the TRA, albeit much diminished and in its last days. The isolated line along the rift valley down the east coast had just been re-gauged and linked to the rest of the TRA network but more than 2000km of 762mm line remained in regular use. Within another decade 90% of it had gone. Yet the extent, the longevity and then the speed of decline of Taiwan's narrow gauge network passed by European railway enthusiasts almost unnoticed.

Until the advent of the Taipei mass-transit system (MRT) in the 1990s, then the Taiwan High Speed Railway in 2006, the whole of Taiwan's railway network was of less than standard gauge (1435mm), predominantly either 1067mm (3ft 6in) or 762mm (2ft 6in). As on railway systems in Japan, South Africa and elsewhere, however, to call the 1067mm gauge 'narrow' is something of a misnomer. Today's TRA network carries over 200 million passengers annually on a loading gauge comparable to that in the UK (York built electric multiple units based on BR's Mk II stock were a mainstay of mainline services until 2008) and apart from branch lines is electrified almost throughout. Fast tilting trains, suburban stopping services and bulk load freight all share the same tracks. TRA's operations are impressive and its management is focussed on operating an intensive service safely and efficiently. It

Opposite: Narrow gauge territory, Taiwan style (2). A winding river that quickly becomes a raging torrent after a typhoon, crossed by a rudimentary wooden bridge with thickly forested mountain slopes rising steeply on either side. Add tight curves and single-bladed point-work and the scene is typical of the lighter industrial lines throughout the country. But for the small loco-tractor with a modern engine seen at the bottom of the picture the scene might have been at almost any time in the last hundred years. Chungkuang mine near Shihfen in the Pingxi valley south east of Taipei in the early 1990s.

John Raby

also has a commendable approach to its heritage and in recent years has returned several steam locomotives to working order as well as preserving old depots and stations. But as the 'standard' operator in Taiwan, it is largely outside the scope of this book, for which purposes 'narrow gauge' means narrower than 1067mm.

While Taiwan did briefly have at least one 3-foot (914mm) gauge line in Keelung docks, in practice this means 762mm gauge or less, known colloquially in Taiwan as *wufenche* (五分車), literally 'half size train' from the gauge being approximately half standard gauge (1435mm). Almost the entire network was developed while Taiwan was a Japanese colony. When Taiwan was annexed in 1895, Japan already had a variety of gauges. But the 762mm gauge was in growing use in Japan so was a logical choice for its overseas colonies, Korea as well as Taiwan. Later it was to become the ruling narrow gauge in China, too. It was a practical choice that stood the test of time well, although private lines also adopted narrower gauges as will be shown.

In addition to the 762mm lines and the push-cart lines, there were a small number of 610mm (2 ft.) gauge industrial lines and narrower, including at least one of 495mm gauge. Collectively this remarkable and fascinating network played a major part in the opening up of Taiwan. A comprehensive history of it, the different lines, the politics and personalities involved, the operations, would be a truly fascinating study. This book is a long way from being that. It is but a brief overview of the system, enough of which remains today to provide ongoing pleasure and interest to railway enthusiasts, but I hope that it may encourage wider interest in the history of both the lines and of Taiwan itself.

A NOTE ON CHINESE NAMES

Confusion often arises when transliterating Taiwanese names and places into Roman script. While China has used the *pinyin* form for many years now and this has become widely accepted, in Taiwan official preference until 2000 was to use the older *Wade-Giles* form. Although an official change was made to *pinyin* in 2008, for practical reasons the Romanised form of most place names continues to be given in the older format. Thus, the capital city is written as Taipei and not Taibei as it would be in *pinyin,* the second city as Kaohsiung, not Gaoxiong and so on. Similarly, many Taiwanese continue to use the *Wade-Giles* form, or even their own private preference, when rendering their name in Roman script. I have attempted to follow current Taiwanese practice throughout but have fallen back on *pinyin* where this is not clear or not established. Where this risks causing confusion, for example because a place name is radically different when written in the two forms, I have added the name in traditional Chinese in brackets.

The view from Zhaoping (originally Alishan) station across the valley. The line of the Mianyue (Monkey Rock) branch can be seen clearly on the far mountainside under an extensive avalanche shelter, showing the extensive civil engineering required for even a secondary line in this territory. Landslide damage to the line from a 1999 earthquake is also evident. 5 May 2016

SWEAT AND TOIL:
THE PUSH-CART LINES

Taiwan is small – somewhat smaller than Switzerland but similarly mountainous, with more than 100 peaks of 3000 metres or higher. It lies at the junction of several tectonic plates, the activity between which has resulted in the formation of a line of mountains that rise steeply from sea level to nearly 4000 metres at their highest point. This mountain chain runs almost the whole length of the island. The rise from seabed to sea level is just as dramatic if less visible. Barely 50 miles offshore the Pacific Trench is as deep as Taiwan's mountains are high. But Taiwan is also very fertile. Despite its small size, the country boasts several distinct climatic zones. The Tropic of Cancer crosses the island and at sea level much of it is tropical and well suited to sugar cultivation. As the height increases, so the vegetation gradually changes to that of sub-tropical zones, then above 2000 metres temperate zones and around the highest summits alpine. Its climate and location are such that an estimated 80% of the crops in the world can grow there. This fertility helps sustain a population more than three times that of Switzerland.

The classic picture of a push-cart line. A scene from a coloured postcard, popular in the 1920s and 1930s, it is a highly stylised view that nonetheless conveys the concept well, including the light construction of civil engineering features, such as the bridge here.

National Central Library of Taiwan

車 台 行 社 露 (灣台)
62. PUSH CAR. FORMOSA.

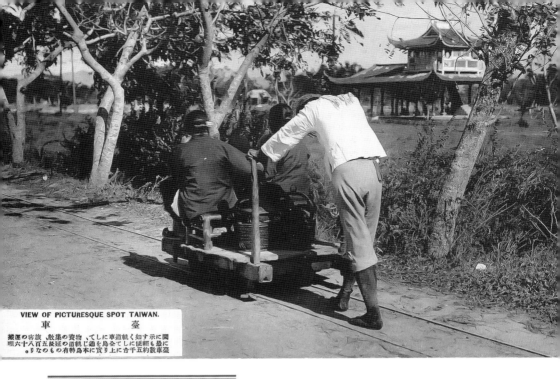

VIEW OF PICTURESQUE SPOT TAIWAN.

臺　車

關に示す如く車道軌じ通を全島に亘り以上に總延べ五千二百六十
關に上に賞し本島に特有のものなり。延道軌じ延長五百八十六
關の物貨の集散、族客の運搬。

A more accurate view of a push-cart in operation. Rather than the two pushers for one passenger seen in the previous picture, one pusher was the norm.

National Central Library of Taiwan

Over time sediments formed through the weathering of the mountain range made a plain down most of the west coast, significantly wider towards the south. This is where most of the island's population, agriculture and general economic activity is concentrated. The mountains remain a formidable barrier today. Just three roads cross the island through them and all are frequently closed by landslides. In 2006 a motorway tunnel was finally blasted through the northern end of the mountain range after years of work. At the time, it was the longest road tunnel in Asia. An 8km long railway tunnel pierces the mountains in the far south on a section of line opened in 1992. The only other rail link between the two sides of the island is around the very northern tip.

Today's Taiwanese are overwhelmingly of ethnic Chinese origin and China still aggressively and noisily claims Taiwan as a province. But aboriginal Taiwanese are ethnically Polynesian and the first outside settlers were Europeans. The island was christened *Ilha Formosa* ('beautiful island') by Portuguese explorers but it was the Dutch who established the strongest foothold. In the early 17th century their East India Company identified the south-western plains as an ideal location for growing sugar cane. Encouraged and assisted by the Dutch, Chinese immigrants came to the island to cultivate the sugar, then later in the century a Chinese pirate leader and warlord, Cheng Cheng-kung, or Koxinga, invaded and expelled the Dutch, intending to use the island as a base from which to try to overthrow the new Qing emperor on the mainland. Instead, the emperor's army invaded the island to defeat the warlord and claimed it for China. Having done so, the imperial court largely ignored or neglected

The adaptability of push-carts is demonstrated well in this picture – place a single seat instead of a box on the chassis and provide some shade from the sun and the humble cart becomes a VIP mode of transport. Mount Kakuban is the Japanese name for Jiaobanshan, close to Taoyuan, south of Taipei.

National Central Library of Taiwan

the island for the next two hundred years. Chinese settlers continued to arrive in small numbers, usually seeking to escape from famine, banditry, government oppression or a combination thereof but even by the mid-19th century they had not moved out of the western lowlands. Most of the island remained occupied solely by different aboriginal tribes and the island generally was considered lawless. Western seafarers shipwrecked there were regularly murdered or sold into slavery. As a later American resident explained

> *Although Formosa was nominally possessed by China, it was well known that over the larger half, that nation claimed no jurisdiction, and that even in the Chinese districts the authority of the emperor was weak and dubious.*[*]

Despite imperial neglect, the island's potential had not gone unnoticed by other countries. In addition to sugar, production of rice and tea was increasing, camphor trees, an important source of ingredients for gunpowder, medicine and anti-oxidants as well as other uses, grew in abundance in lowland forests and coal and gold were being mined around Keelung, north east of Taipei. All these and more were being

---

* James W Davidson: *The Island of Formosa Past and Present*, London, 1903.

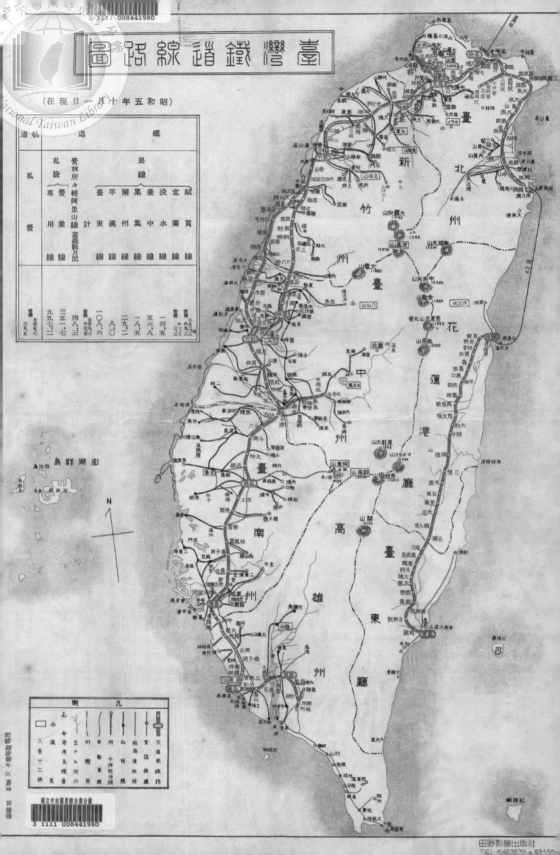

Opposite: The Taiwan railway network in 1930. The map shows clearly not only the extent of the push-cart network (shown by black hatched lines on the map) but also how railways penetrated deep into the interior of the country despite the forbidding terrain. Solid black lines are sugar mill railways.

National Taiwan Library

shipped to China when in 1858 the Imperial Court agreed to open the island to foreign trade. In 1861 Great Britain opened the first consulate. Other countries were more ambitious: in 1874 Japan occupied part of the south seeking retribution after 54 of its sailors were murdered following a shipwreck on the island, then in 1884 the French bombarded Keelung. This latter incident appears to have persuaded the court in Beijing to heed the advice of their Commissioner on Formosa to make the island a province under direct rule rather than as an adjunct of mainland Fujian (or Fukien). The Commissioner, Liu Ming-chuan, was duly appointed the first governor and Taiwan became a province in 1887. Liu immediately embarked upon a programme of infrastructure development and general modernisation.

Keelung was the only port on the island readily accessible by ocean going steamers as opposed to sailing ships and Liu received permission from the Imperial government to build a railway from there down the west coast with the eventual aim of reaching the former administrative centre at what is now Tainan. A British consulting engineer, H. C. Matheson, was appointed, work started in 1887 and the first 11-mile section was opened in 1889. At the time the 'Cape gauge' of 3ft 6in or 1067mm was being widely adopted overseas, not only in southern Africa but New Zealand, parts of Australia and neighbouring Japan, so its selection here was uncontroversial. Rails of 36lb/yard were used. Contemporary accounts suggest it was both poorly and cheaply constructed, nevertheless except for a short-lived line in Shanghai in the 1870s, this was the first railway line to be built in Imperial China and the first transport infrastructure of any sort on Taiwan. Keelung was reached in 1891 and Hsinchu, south of Taipei, in 1893, giving a route length of almost 100km. Liu Ming-chuan had resigned on health grounds in 1891, however, and in 1893 the government stopped further work on harbour development in Keelung. The railway proceeded no further and without Liu's enterprise and drive the growth of Taiwan stagnated and the railway quickly started to deteriorate.[*]

In 1894 China and Japan fought a brief war from which the latter emerged victorious and under the terms of the settlement gained control of Taiwan. The agreement was not popular with the few elite on the island who made a half-hearted effort to declare an independent republic. Banditry and lawlessness were rife while the eastern side of the island was largely unexplored and firmly in the hands of various aboriginal tribes. Apart from the railway line, communications throughout the island were rudimentary at best. Roads were almost non-existent, most travel being by boat. The immediate priority for the Japanese was to pacify the island, for which improved communications were essential so as to be able to move troops around quickly. Completion of the railway line down the west coast was the first requirement, starting with a full rebuilding of the existing line on a new alignment. Although relatively straightforward, a section in the hills north of Taichung required several tunnels. Many rivers also had to be

---

[*] Matheson recounted his experiences as consulting engineer in *Railways in China, Minutes of the Proceedings of the Institute Of Civil Engineers, vol cix*. One of the original locomotives for the line, a German built 0-4-0, is preserved in the National Museum in Taipei

Even push-cart lines could not avoid heavy engineering in the most challenging areas. This view is in the south of the island, near to Tainan.

National Central Library of Taiwan

crossed. These were wide and for most of the year shallow or even dry beds that turned into raging torrents after the frequent typhoons, so there was no alternative to lengthy viaducts across them. All this required capital but the Japanese expectation was that the new colony would finance its own needs. In any case Japan was hardly in a position to finance major new investment in the colony. The war had both drained the government's coffers and left it with domestic financial problems, so completion of the line proved to be unexpectedly protracted.

Following the occupation, the Japanese army had brought with it wagons and track for a Decauville designed hand-powered 500mm system. This had been intended for use very much as originally designed, as a light, portable but robust transport system for moving munitions and other material to the front line in a war. In the aftermath of the Japanese occupation it was used in this way as troops were moved about the island to try to restore order. Usually troops would land at a point on the coast from where they would lay tracks some kilometres inland as needed. But as order was gradually imposed, the equipment was pressed into service as a stop-gap to plug gaps in the main railway link while this was still being constructed. For a short while, the entire distance between Hsinchu, southern terminus of the steam railway, and Kaohsiung was linked by a long push-cart line – probably the longest such line anywhere, ever. As the 1067mm gauge line was extended, so this push-cart line was gradually replaced. The final section, across the Dajia river north of Taichung, lasted until completion of the bridge here in 1907, the final link in the west coast line, and proved to be a sophisticated operation. A long timber trestle viaduct was first constructed across the river bed and a double track push-cart system was then laid on this. But this was considerably lower than the level of the railway line on either side, so to gain height on the southern side a series of loops had to be built to keep the gradient at a manageable slope.

On completion of the 1067mm track such temporary lines were no longer necessary. But their success in meeting a short-term need proved inspirational. The Japanese government was anxious to exploit the island's resources, not least to raise the funds to pay for its 'pacification' programme. But the infrastructure to access the resources was non-existent. Other than the newly completed railway, the only way of moving about on land was on a series of footpaths, often rough and narrow being primarily intended for farmers to access their crops. They were completely unsuitable for the transport of large amounts of natural resources, such as coal or timber. But the geography of Taiwan was challenging and the Japanese economy was going through difficulties at the turn of the century, so raising large amounts of capital to invest in infrastructure was out of the question. The Decauville lines on the other hand had already demonstrated both their practicality and economy. A track could be laid in little more space than that taken by the existing network of footpaths between paddy fields, so earthworks would be minimal and bridges could be built from locally available materials at little cost, while the initial rails and rolling stock already existed *in situ*. These went on to form the basis of an ultimately extensive and long-lived network of push-cart lines, the last of which survived into the 1970s, indeed the concept survived in limited use into the 1990s in some coal mines.

The push-carts, known locally as *tai-che* (台車, literally, 'platform car') were a singularly Taiwanese institution and that they proved to be so extensive in range and long-lasting was very much a reflection of the circumstances of the island.

Although derived from Decauville's portable railway principles and designed for temporary operations, the push-cart lines proved remarkably long lived. This view was on the very last, still operating in the Taipei suburb of Wudu in early 1976 (see also Chapter 6).

Nicholas Pertwee

A QUESTION OF GAUGE – 1

As originally designed, Decauville's portable railway system used two gauges, 500mm and 600mm, with the former intended primarily but not exclusively for hand operated lines and the latter intended more for ones using locomotives. Most Taiwanese publications about the push-cart lines quote 500mm as the normal gauge, as does Charles Small in his books. Strictly speaking, it should be 495mm. In 1909 the Railway Department of the Japanese Government General recorded gauges for the first time and noted that 82% of push-cart lines were of 495mm gauge and the remainder of 610mm gauge. By 1914 2ft. 6in. (762mm) was also recorded as being used for some lines. Interestingly, the gauges were all recorded in Imperial measures (feet and inches), not metric measures or traditional Taiwanese measurements, similar to Japanese *kanejaku*, in which one *chi* (尺) or foot is 303mm. Quibbling over a difference of 5mm might be seen as the ultimate example of pedantry, especially as most lines were fairly crudely built so gauges were hardly likely to be precise. But by 1928 the Railway Department's records listed another five gauges used for push-carts, varying from 406mm to 545mm. Taiwanese scholar Dr Chen Chia Hao argues that these were most probably mistakes in recording – for example, 545mm is 1ft. 9½in. while 495mm is 1ft. 7½in. and a 7 might frequently be mistaken for a 9, especially in handwritten documents. This is certainly plausible, especially as the government used Arabic numerals (0-9) in its documents at a time when Chinese numerals were still commonly used in everyday life (railway timetables were in exclusively Chinese script until 1949 if not later). Indeed, the official records provide a good example of the problem – those for 1922 list the two push-cart gauges as 17.5 and 20, which might reasonably be taken to mean inches until one compares the 1923 records where they are shown as 1'7.5" and 2'0" (1ft. 7½in. and 2ft.)! Another likely error is over how the actual measurements were made – whether from the inside of each rail or the middle or even outside. We have no way of knowing.

But it was not just a matter of mis-recording. The former push-cart line at Wulai (see Chapter 6) is of 545mm gauge and in conducting research for this book I discovered a long-abandoned and half-buried section of track in the Taichung suburb of Tuniu, also of 545mm gauge (see chapter 4). The rebuilt section of the Wudu line at Luliao (see also Chapter 6) is approximately 475mm gauge but that in the nearby museum at Tungshan is a few millimetres wider. My assumption is that given the level of development in Taiwan in the early 20th century, standard measures were unlikely to be enforced or even generally adopted and the rolling stock for push-cart lines could be and probably usually was easily and commonly made by local carpenters and blacksmiths. There was therefore very probably significant variation in the gauge of different push-cart lines, possibly on a regional basis. Furthermore, a precise gauge was not of paramount importance with such basic stock and low speeds. Measurement of extant push-cart rail at Jingtong station in the Pingxi valley (also in Chapter 6) revealed a variation in the gauge of up to 1.5cm within a space of a few metres.

Small in *Rails to the Mines* rightly talks therefore of a 'theoretical 500mm'. He also writes of rails being turned on their side to be used once the head had worn down, or being replaced by angle iron! So, references to 495mm gauge, or indeed any gauge narrower than 610mm, should be considered as indicative, not definitive.

A permanent way train. Taken on the Keelung Coal Co. Railway line rather than the adjacent Yourui push-cart line, this is nevertheless a latter day photo of a push-cart in operation. Wudu, 1976.

Nicholas Pertwee

Transport development in most European countries had evolved and adapted over many centuries: Roman era roads formed the basis of later turnpikes or post roads, rivers and canals offered inland transport before giving way over time to railways. Taiwan in 1900 had almost none of these, shoals and rapids making most of its rivers unnavigable over anything more than very short stretches and most inland travel was on foot. In the middle of the 19th century an overland journey from Tamsui in the north to Tainan, around 350km, would take around 19 days. In these conditions the impact of the push-carts was dramatic. It is no exaggeration to compare the impact they had on Taiwan's development with that of the railways in mid-19th century Great Britain. By providing access to the main railway line and in turn to the ports, they increased the area under agricultural development and they opened up new mines and camphor wood forests. And from the government perspective, they facilitated the movement of troops and officials to control and manage the population.

Their attractiveness lay in their simplicity and low cost. Rails of around 9lb/yard could be lifted and moved by small numbers of men, yet a loaded push-cart could carry some 200kg. of freight or four passengers at speeds of around 9km/hour on the level, faster downhill. To begin with routes were all single track but an empty push-cart was light enough simply to be lifted off the rails to allow a loaded one to pass in the other direction and soon a code of etiquette was established under which this became the norm. Signalling and other elements that might add to the construction or operating costs were therefore unnecessary. At its most basic, a cart was simply a platform on four wheels, with a pole in each corner to facilitate pushing, by one or two persons depending on load and gradient and from either direction. On to this platform a rudimentary box could be placed to make a passenger cart, or for VIPs more comfortable chairs and even roofs could be added or removed as required. Civil engineering work could similarly be kept to a minimum. It was far from unknown for passengers to have to get off and walk across riverbeds because the trestle carrying the railway was considered insufficiently strong to take their additional weight.

Despite these attractions, push-cart lines did not immediately take off. Although they may have been quick, cheap and simple to construct, the new government had brought with it a policy of strong central control, including wanting to manage and oversee communications. The main west coast railway, for example, initially privately owned, was taken over by the government in 1907. And as we shall see in subsequent chapters, a similar attitude towards control extended to other railways. But local enterprise, taking the now redundant military lines and carts and using them initially on a very local basis, started to demonstrate their potential.

By 1910 the island's government accepted that neither it nor Japanese settlers had the wherewithal to develop infrastructure on their own and the regulations for managing push-cart lines were relaxed. Local mayors were actively encouraged to promote them and franchises for operating them were offered to local Taiwanese, under which the basic infrastructure and equipment would be provided by the local government which also set the fares, with companies then paying for their use. The effect was dramatic. From only 267km in 1909 – less than the 436km length of the west coast 1067mm railway – the push-cart system grew quickly, to 1087km in 1916. There was then a dip in track mileage before a further change in regulations in 1922 led the system to grow to its maximum extent of 1367km in 1931. The peak year for traffic was 1927, when more than 5.3 million passengers and 840,000 tonnes of freight were carried. The main items of the latter, at least in the 1920s, were basic materials for construction and livelihood: stone and gravel, rice and timber in that order, all bulk products that would be better suited to road transport as soon as it was available.

By 1934 there were 62 push-cart railway companies. The smallest controlled a line just 1.2km long, the largest a network of 104km with 550 push-carts. In the early years, traffic was heaviest in the Tainan area in the south. In 1922 one company in this area carried over 300,000 passengers but in due course this was overtaken by the region around Taipei, where in 1934 the largest company carried half a million passengers and 150,000 tonnes of freight on its 45km of track. The most common gauge was 495mm (1ft 7½in) or thereabouts, in 1922 just three lines of 610mm gauge being recorded and one of 762mm (but see the box in this chapter), generally using rails of 9lb/yard (approximately 4.5kg/metre) although 12lb/yard was not unusual. One line in Tainan was recorded as using 18lb/yard rail. This may have been a genuine reflection of the volumes of traffic carried given the initial demand in this area, or it may just be a recording error.

The system at Wulai to the south of Taipei, which is described in more detail in Chapter 6 may not be typical but nonetheless it illustrates well the general pattern. The first line in the area was built soon after the turn of the century in connection with a privately financed Japanese hydro-electric project. Economic difficulties in Japan

鐵道文史

Forty years after the last working push-cart line in the country closed, small museums at either end provide reminders of what was once a major mode of transport in the country. This is a replica push-cart, fitted with a box for passenger services, in the Tungshan Museum, Wudu, 11 September 2016.

At the far end of what was once the Yourui push-cart line the local government has built a short section of track on which a visiting Japanese tourist tries his hand at pushing a replica cart, Wudu 11 September 2016.

around 1904 meant the family behind the scheme was unable to raise more funds for further development. The push-cart line remained however, and was extended a short way to a nearby settlement, improving communications (whether by local initiative or the original Japanese investors is not clear). After 1910 the line was extended further north towards Xindian, a short way south of Taipei. Then, after the Mitsui Corporation was given a licence to start logging in the Wulai area in 1921 the system expanded greatly, first north to Xindian, then south to Fushan, deep in the mountains, and over time with a series of branch lines into side valleys. In 1922 a private railway was built south from Taipei to Xindian, providing a connection there with the push-cart network. At first the 'main line' between here and Wulai was upgraded, but by the start of the Second World War a road had been built as far as Wulai and the line between here and Xindian ceased operations. In the ensuing years as roads were built or forests cleared, most of the branch lines also closed but the southernmost section as far as Fushan was still in use and carrying passengers into the 1960s when a Taiwanese friend remembers using it for going on university fieldwork trips.

Both route length and traffic started to decline from the beginning of the 1930s. The very success of the lines in stimulating growth encouraged road construction the better to cope with growing demand, bringing with it competition from trucks, buses and pedal transport. But as this happened, so the very adaptability of the Decauville system meant that lines were frequently lifted and redeployed to previously inaccessible locations, thereby encouraging further growth.

From the government's perspective, the primary aim of the lines was to contribute to the growth of the colony through helping to finance its own development while also contributing to that of Japan itself. But by opening operation of them to Taiwanese, the lines were also to play a significant role in the rise of domestic enterprise. To begin with, a family or small group of families might have joined forces to finance one or two lines. But lines or companies soon combined so that one company might operate several lines in a particular area. Taiwan hitherto had been a primarily agricultural economy but in this way the seeds of modern enterprise and capital formation were well and truly sown. The terms of the concessions granted to Taiwanese were generous, enabling several of the firms to accumulate substantial funds from the profits they made. In time some of the companies expanded to operate conventional railways or more frequently bus and road transport companies, becoming leading enterprises in the regions within which they operated and laying the base for subsequent economic expansion and further development.

Nor was it only the elites who benefited. To the modern mind the concept of human powered transport may seem uncomfortably reminiscent of slave labour. But in what had been until then a predominantly subsistence economy, where the margin between survival and starvation could depend on the annual harvest, pushing carts offered one of the first opportunities for earning a cash income, certainly more attractive than being an agricultural day labourer. One of the very earliest push-cart operators recalled it as being a steady job with relatively good working conditions and income by the standards of the time.* Furthermore, by providing reasonable access to markets

---

*   Conversation with Luo Shui-lian (羅水連), Houli, 24 April 2016. His grandfather worked on construction of the initial west coast line at Tai'an while the permanent line was being built across the Dajia river here, then later as a push-cart operator. He recalled his grandfather saying initial

Almost certainly the most famous push-cart line in the country is the one that takes sightseers to the waterfalls south of Wulai in the Taipei suburbs. Now fully mechanised, a short stretch of demonstration track including a turntable and replica cart, survives at the Falls station. The rudimentary brake handles can be clearly seen in this picture, in addition to the corner poles for pushing the cart (see also Chapter 6) Wulai, 21 May 2016.

for the first time, farmers had an incentive to produce more crops than they needed for their own consumption as they were able to sell the surplus, further helping the spread of industrialisation and urbanisation.

The push-cart lines were not evenly spread over the island. They predominated in the north and the western central areas. There were relatively few on the east coast, mainly because the population here was small and scattered. In the south, for reasons explained in the next chapter, many more lines were 762mm gauge and locomotive operated. Notwithstanding their adaptability in being re-deployed to new areas as roads opened, their use declined steadily during the 1930s as the road network expanded. But it was a steady decline, not a rapid one: more than two million passengers were carried in 1938, after which there was a temporary resurgence in traffic due to fuel shortages during and after the 2nd World War. In 1940 official

conditions when building the line were hard, possibly tantamount to forced labour but after he became a push-cart operator pay and conditions were much better and a big improvement on life in Chinese days.

records showed over 3600 push-carts in service on some 960km of lines although how intensively they were used is not known.

That the decline should continue during the 1950s was inevitable. But it was slow and steady rather than dramatic. Only by the middle of the decade had the network fallen back to the same length it had been in 1909. Push-carts were slow, expensive compared to road traffic and redolent of a bygone era but many mountain areas remained without road access. More surprising perhaps was that they remained popular in many suburban areas, their frequency and convenience offsetting the slowness and lack of comfort. It was also a reflection not only of the lack of private cars but also the wider inadequacy of public transport at the time. In the chaos of the immediate post-war years this had often all but ceased functioning and it was only in the 1960s that a fully adequate service started to be commonplace.

Although the end was inevitable, the last few lines were slow to go. Mention has already been made of the Wulai system which continued as a push-cart line until 1963. Official statistics recorded 46.6km of lines still in use the previous year and nearly 40km as late as 1970, mostly in the Hualien area, still isolated from the main rail and road network at this date. But the very last line in use was not in a remote mountain region but in the eastern Taipei suburb of Wudu, where the Yourui line continued in operation until the mid-1970s. By this time the Keelung-Taipei motorway had been built through Wudu and the Yourui line passed under it in a specially built underbridge, surely the only place in the world where a motorway has crossed such a line. Both this line and that at Wulai are covered further in Chapter 6.

2

THE SUGAR MILL RAILWAYS

Early Years

Unlikely though it may now seem, Taiwan was once the world's fourth largest sugar producer, after India, Cuba and Java. Production dates back to at least the 17th century, when the Dutch had started the industry in the broad plains in the south west of the island, where the combination of flat, fertile land and considerable annual rainfall made for ideal growing conditions. It grew in importance as a cash crop, already mainly exported to Japan, under Chinese rule. But the global importance of the industry only came after the Japanese occupied the island after 1895 and more particularly once the 1905 war with Russia was over. Growing prosperity in Japan saw a changing diet, including a rapid increase in sugar consumption. It was already one of the five biggest imports so the Japanese were quick to make the most of the potential offered by their new colony to meet this growing demand. Annual production grew from some tens of thousands of tons at the turn of the century to a peak of 1.4 million tons by 1939.

An old postcard view of the first mill built in the Japanese period at Qiaotou in what is now modern Kaohsiung, showing locos no 1 (Porter 3832), 3 (Porter 3834) and what is probably no 2 (Porter 3833), all of 1907.

Author's collection

Ehou mill of the Taiwan Sugar company, (modern day Pingtung) with two mixed trains in the station. The loco heading the train on the left is no 5, a 6.5t Porter 0-4-0ST, builder's no. 4037 of 1907. The loco on the right appears to be one of two 0-8-0T 17.5t Henschels of 1908, builder's number 8868 or 8869, running number 10 or 11. Note the 1067mm gauge siding on the extreme left of the picture.

Author's collection

The very first locos on the sugar lines came from American suppliers, closely followed by British ones in the form of Avonside and Andrew Barclay. But over time the most successful non-Japanese suppliers were German, above all Orenstein & Koppel. The locomotive in this particular shot is not identified but the outline is of distinctly German lineage.

National Central Library of Taiwan

The smallest 762mm gauge locos supplied for sugar mill work in Taiwan were a trio of diminutive 5 ton 0-4-0s delivered to Taiwan Sugar's Eiko or Sankandian mill at Yongkang, north of Tainan, probably from Orenstein & Koppel. The loco's size and running number both point to this being one of them.

Robin Gibbons' collection

In marked contrast to the years of neglect Taiwan had suffered under Chinese Imperial rule, the Japanese were quick to make a comprehensive survey of the island's resources and potential. In 1896 Dr Nitobe Inazo, a graduate of American and German universities, was appointed to head the new Industry Bureau, which included responsibility for both agriculture and forestry. Over the next five years he drew up detailed plans for agricultural development, including very detailed proposals for how the government would help private Japanese companies develop the sugar industry. In recent years the term 'public-private partnership' has become common in the UK but the concept if not the term was already familiar to the Japanese one hundred years earlier. Actual development of the industry was left to private enterprise but operating within a policy framework and guidelines set by the state. The first Japanese company to be involved, known as both the Formosan Sugar Company and Taiwan Sugar Company was established in 1900. It included members of the Imperial Household and the Mitsui family among its investors and as a sweetener the government also subsidised 6% of the overall capital investment. Other entrepreneurs soon followed and the government ensured that large areas of land were turned over to sugar production.

The first sugar mill in the colonial period opened at Qiaotou, north of what is now the second city of Kaohsiung, in 1901. More mills soon followed. By 1915 there were 35 of them, operated by 13 companies. Modern, large scale mills were the order of the day from the outset, requiring major capital investment. So, in marked contrast

Seasonal peaks in demand during harvesting meant that steam power could still be seen on sugar trains throughout the 1970s despite the steady introduction of diesel traction. Here TSC no 370 (Tubize 2354 of 1948), then based at Annei mill near Chiayi, heads a loaded sugar train. The tank behind the loco was a supplementary water tank, a common sight on the sugar lines. The loco has been preserved and can be seen today working occasional special trains at Wushulin mill east of Chiayi.

Nicholas Pertwee

to the push-cart network this was an industry dominated by Japanese interests, to which the government gave preference. Initially each mill and accompanying land for growing cane was allotted to a different company but government policy and behaviour encouraged mergers and takeovers so that by 1939 there were 43 mills but only eight companies. In practice the industry was dominated by four large Japanese corporations: the Enshuiko, Meiji, Dai Nippon (also known as Nitto Kogyo) and Taiwan (or Formosa) sugar companies, each of which eventually operated several mills as a result of takeovers and mergers. By 1939 these four groups accounted for 94% of all production.

The industrial scale of production was quite new to Taiwan. It required effective means of transport both to bring the raw sugar cane to the mills and to get the refined sugar to market, primarily in Japan. This meant a rail network in both cases, to bring the cane from the fields and a connection either to the west coast railway or to the nearest suitable port. In this respect, the sugar lines were not very different to those in other major sugar producing countries. Initially they also relied on push-cart lines to bring cane from the fields, using both human power and water buffalo traction. From the outset, some of the largest mills also built 1067mm gauge industrial branch lines or sidings to connect to the government railway where this could be done at low cost, usually because of proximity. It was not long before human and buffalo motive power

Beigang station west of Chiayi, showing the substantial facilities common to the busier stations. The main station building is in the far background, behind the railcar which is on an express service to Chiayi. The loco at the island platform is no 715, an Orenstein & Koppel 0-8-0T. It spent almost all its working life at Beigang but despite receiving a major overhaul in 1964, was not one of the many locos surviving into preservation. A rake of early wooden bodied 4-wheel passenger carriages is in the siding on the extreme left. 6 March 1966.

M Umemura

was seen to be wholly inadequate for the needs of a large mill and early moves were made to adopt steam traction, the first recorded deliveries being 3 locomotives from HK Porter of the USA, two 10 ton 0-4-0 saddle tanks and a larger 13.5 ton 0-6-0, builder's numbers 3832-4. These arrived in Taiwan in November 1907 for service at the Qiaotou mill. From then on, mechanisation proceeded steadily, albeit not uniformly. Early railway maps of Taiwan show many of the lines close to mills as push-cart lines, and particularly for smaller mills locomotive haulage came later. A case in point is the mill at Puli, in the centre of the country, which opened in 1912. The Taiwan archives have records of hand-powered trolleys from the mill, suggesting the operation started as a hand-cart line before locos were introduced, possibly on the same gauge.

Expansion of the main sugar cane rail network was rapid, moving ahead even of construction of the main west coast railway. By December 1908 five separate sugar companies had already built more than 320km of line, with public services offered over 140km. Another 240km were planned or under construction. The *Far Eastern Review* noted that by December 1910, there were 55 steam locomotives in use on the sugar mill lines but buffalo haulage was also still widespread. Contemporary photos show buffalos much in evidence for hauling cut cane from the fields, which would be logical given both the seasonal nature of this work and the relatively light rails used in the fields. While steam locomotives are also shown on this work, it is probable that in the early years they were used mainly on public trains and for shipping the refined sugar from the mills. The official statistics record the different categories of line separately and in the 1920s nearly 40 push-cart lines were listed as being operated

A QUESTION OF GAUGE - 2

As noted in the introduction, the 762mm gauge was already in use in Japan at the time of annexation. But it was far from being universal. According to Small, the Imperial Army alone used five different ones and as if that was not enough, its Osaka Arsenal had a system on yet another gauge, the comparatively unusual one of 950mm. 762mm was adopted as the normal gauge for the lines in the Imperial Forests at Kiso and Tsugaru. But the timing of its introduction here is not clear – the system in Kiso Forest was hand-powered until 1907 when it was rebuilt and mechanised. It is not clear if the gauge was changed at the same time. All the main Taiwan sugar mills adopted the gauge for their rail networks, however, with one notable exception. This was the mill at Puli which, as noted above, started operations with hand powered tramways. At a time when all other mills were ordering 762mm gauge locos from overseas, however, this mill opted for the 610mm gauge, ordering two Andrew Barclay and two Orenstein & Koppel 0-4-0Ts. (The Barclays were works nos 1263 and 1264 of 1911). Why this mill should have been the exception is not clear. It is purely supposition on my part but the mill was located in the centre of the island, in marginal land for sugar cultivation, so it may have been one of the few built by Taiwanese enterprise with the owners not sharing the same inclination to a common gauge as did the Japanese corporations. The line was still 610mm gauge on nationalisation under the TSC but was re-gauged soon after and a 762mm gauge loco which used to operate here is now preserved at the mill at Xihu.

by sugar mills. Many of these were almost certainly no more than light tramways to provide access into the cane fields; the Taiwan Sugar Company was listed as having eight push-cart lines for example but the longest was barely 3km and some were just hundreds of metres in length. On the other hand, the mill at Shuigang in what is now Kaohsiung was shown as having one push-cart line of over 11km even in 1922.

The sugar lines differed in one very important aspect from those in other countries. From the outset, several of the lines went beyond the immediate needs of the sugar mill they served by providing common carrier services, in almost all cases in the form of feeder services to and from the main government railway. In this way communications were opened up to more parts of the island than would have been feasible through the government railway network alone. Although privately run, these common carrier lines formed an integral part of the island's public transport network, comprising a distinct second tier of services after the government's first tier 1067mm network (which in total length of around 800km was itself not much larger than the public sugar lines) with a third tier provided by the push-cart tramways. Operations on these lines therefore had to reflect three distinct requirements: the provision of year-round public services, transport of sugar to ports or markets, and the seasonal transport of cane from the fields to the mills. Separate government regulations applied to the common carrier sugar lines and the push-cart lines and for the most part the gauges of the two networks remained distinct as, too, did the ownership structure. As already noted, Taiwanese owned companies were prominent in push-cart line development whereas they were largely squeezed out of the sugar industry and associated railway systems.

The background to the provision of common carrier services is not clear. They may have been an explicit condition of the early concessions for opening mills and devoting large areas to sugar cultivation; sugar companies may have offered to run them in the hope of securing more attractive concession terms; or they may simply have been run as a profitable side-line to the main business. While the position seems to have differed between mills, the evidence points to the first possibility. Early maps showing the lines on which public services were provided correspond closely with the specific areas in which concessions were allocated, with generally one public service line in each concession area. Nor was there any expansion of the common carrier network after the initial flurry of such lines was constructed up to the mid-1920s, lending support to the thesis that this was a public service obligation, although expansion of the island's road network from the same period probably made further lines unnecessary. In post-war years, the Sugar Corporation's network maps clearly delineate 'sugar lines [run] for government railways' – a strong indication that by then at least the passenger services were a social obligation run at government behest.

Evidence of reluctance to meet obligations also comes from the construction of the Taiwan Sugar Company's line from Chiuchutang (九曲堂) the then planned terminus of a ten mile branch at the southern end of the government's 1067mm gauge west coast railway, up the valley of the Chishan river to Chishan (旗山) and beyond. The railway was originally intended to go for almost 80km north along the river valley but never got further than half way, suggesting a compromise agreement with the government was quietly reached.

Whatever reluctance there may have been, however, the common carrier services were never simply an afterthought or add-on to the principal business of moving sugar. Although they were never provided over more than 630km of a total sugar railway route network of 2900km, trains operated on full published timetables and services could be intensive. The first such service started in 1909 between Xinying and Yanshui and the busiest network was that of the Meiji company which in 1922 carried 760,000 passengers and 59,000 tons of general freight, mainly on two lines between Chiayi and Suantou and further south between Xinying, Longtian and Chiali. Four other companies all carried more than 250,000 passengers the same year. At the peak, there were 600 trains carrying 60,000 passengers daily and 6 million tons of freight annually and the facilities provided were commensurate with such a level of service. There were only 41 stations at most but these were no rudimentary halts, boasting platforms (the larger stations several) complete with awnings and other facilities. Initially at least most lines also maintained distinct locomotive fleets for these services, possibly because of government regulations or more likely because of the different operating requirements.

The size of these separate fleets gives some indication of the relative importance of the public services to different companies. In 1922 for example, the Taiwan Sugar Company had just 5 locos for its public trains but 27 for its own traffic, while the Meiji Company had 14 locos for public services and just 16 for its own traffic. Two smaller companies had more locomotives for public traffic than for their own, suggesting possibly that in these cases the sugar mills were an adjunct to the railway rather than the other way round.

Thus, for most mills the rail network comprised a 'main' line, almost always to a point on the government network, over which public services as well as milled sugar and other products would be carried, and a secondary network, fanning out from the

TSC 366 approaches Suantou mill with a loaded sugar train, May 1979. This loco has been preserved on static display at Hualien sugar mill.

Nicholas Pertwee

mill and over which cut cane would be brought to the mill for crushing. Again, the Meiji company provides a good example, with a total of around 250km of track in 1922 but public services offered over just 110km, on four separate lines, the longest of them 40km. Initially the networks were all separate but as companies merged or were taken over, so in some areas lines were gradually linked, forming the basis of what would eventually become a sprawling, circuitous but connected network. Some of the sugar mills also operated push-cart lines including as common carrier operations.

The industry continued to expand after the first wave of investment as more areas of the island were opened up to development and as demand for sugar continued to grow. This was not only for human consumption. From the 1930s Japan was aggressively pursuing military campaigns overseas, first in Manchuria, then the rest of China and ultimately in the 2nd World War. Ethanol and alcohol production grew in importance accordingly, both to use in explosives manufacture and for transport use. Inevitably this aspect of the industry grew even more important after the outbreak of the 2nd World War. To help meet this growing demand, two new mills were brought into production in the mid-1930s. Of the 41 mills or refineries in production in 1935, the great majority were in the western or south western counties but four were on the east coast, where suitable land was scarce and one was well inland at Puli, the geographical centre of the island. The last new mill opened in December 1946.

The motive power fleet grew commensurately. After the initial flurry of orders, deliveries fell off until 1920 but between then and 1941 the number of locos designated for field and yard work more than doubled, from 109 to 221. By contrast, the fleet dedicated to common carrier services hardly changed in size, rising from 55 in 1920 to a peak of 58 in 1929, falling to a low of 50 in 1937 before rising again to 58 in 1941, evidence perhaps of a lack of enthusiasm for running such services although it may also have reflected a gradual move away from dedicated motive power for such services amid growing standardisation. Certainly in later years locomotives, steam and diesel, appear to have been used interchangeably on both common carrier and dedicated sugar hauling duties.

The mills with 1067mm gauge lines appear to have followed what was by then an already well-established practice of buying second hand locomotives where possible. In 1952 the Taiwan Sugar Corporation or TSC (a state-owned enterprise created after the war and not to be confused with the earlier private company of the same name), under which all the mills had been nationalised following the war, decided to re-number its fleet on a new standard basis. To do this it first compiled a list of all the known locos that had been delivered to the sugar lines. It was an eclectic list, especially for the 1067mm gauge where it reflected the relative strength of British manufacturers in the mid to late 19th century. For it included a Sharp Stewart 2-4-0T of 1875 and two Beyer Peacock tanks of 1894 built for the Imperial Japanese Railways, a Nasmyth Wilson tank of 1892 originally supplied to the Tokyo Water Works railway, and an 1893 2-6-2 Hawthorn Leslie saddle tank, one of 6 delivered new to the original government railway on Taiwan. Sadly, none have survived.

Similar second hand options were not available on the 762mm gauge. Japanese locomotive manufacture was in its infancy in the first decade of the 20th century and as noted, the first locomotives came from the USA, the Porter deliveries of 1907 being followed in 1908 by ones from Baldwin. But a variety of overseas manufacturers responded to demand, Alco and Davenport in the USA winning tenders in addition to

By the late 1970s passenger traffic on TSC lines was in free fall and down to a handful of services. But the fortunate enthusiast could still experience a ride on one and behind steam to boot. Here TSC no 363 (AFB 2651 of 1948) from Suantou mill prepares to head an evening passenger train out of Chiayi in January 1978. The loco has been preserved in Japan.

Nicholas Pertwee

Porter and Baldwin. Tubize in Belgium, Henschel in Germany and Andrew Barclay, Avonside and Kerr Stuart in the UK all supplied locomotives but no other European suppliers came close to matching deliveries from Orenstein & Koppel, who delivered at least 30 locomotives to Taiwanese customers between 1910 and 1930. The first Japanese built locomotive was delivered to a Dai Nippon mill in 1910 and from then on Japanese companies started to predominate in orders, although Baldwin won a further contract in 1920 as well as the O&K orders mentioned. Intriguingly too, Alco of the USA delivered some 22 ton 0-8-0Ts in 1920. Built for the 1067mm gauge, they appear to have been used for construction of a hydro-electric project before being sold to the mill at Ershui and converted to 762mm gauge. None of these early locos survive. The oldest 762mm gauge one preserved today in Taiwan was supplied in 1920.

At this stage the mills were most probably buying 'off-the-shelf' from builders' catalogues. Works order records show a high proportion of these early locomotives as being delivered to agents in either Taiwan or Japan, who presumably would be promoting products to the mills on the basis of the catalogues. In placing their orders,

The year is 1981 and steam is on the way out everywhere, so the photographer's attention is on 2-8-0 DT604 shunting in Chiayi station and the TSC passenger train headed by an unidentified Diema diesel leaves almost unnoticed from the adjacent narrow gauge platforms. But the narrow gauge passenger train would be consigned to history within a matter of weeks while steam would linger on TRA for nearly another two years.

John Raby

the mills appear to have indulged in some possibly unconscious preferences for certain countries or suppliers. For example, Qiaotou mill opted for US manufacturers, whereas the large Enshuikou mill at Xinying north of Tainan, which started railway operations in 1909, chose locos from Avonside and Andrew Barclay of Great Britain, perhaps to go with the second hand British locomotives on its 1067mm gauge lines.[*]

Photographs of the mills at this time show locos of fairly standard industrial design, those from the US being predominantly saddle tanks, either 0-4-0STs or 0-6-0STs. But the 1952 sugar corporation list records 17 0-4-0Ts inherited, 29 0-4-2Ts and a number of 0-4-4Ts. The Orenstein & Koppel Works list alone records 16 0-4-0Ts supplied to Taiwanese customers between 1910 and 1926. Behind the wheel arrangements lay a further variety of locomotive in terms of weight and capacity, the same 1952 list recording eight different sizes of 0-4-0 alone, varying from 3 to 13 tons in weight. To some extent these differences were a natural consequence of the

---

[*]   3 ten ton Avonside 0-6-0s, builder's nos. 1556-8 were delivered in 1908 and a further 5 up to 1915 (works numbers 1577, 1588, 1608, 1609 and 1732).

The loco shed at Huwei Mill, 5 March 1966, with steam power still predominant. Note the dual gauge track in the foreground.

M Umemura

varying requirements: for yard and field work, for passenger services and for loaded cane trains. As familiarity with requirements and operations grew however, so too did a clear preference for either 0-6-0 or 0-6-2 tank engines of increasingly standard designs. TSC inherited 37 of the former and 48 of the latter upon nationalisation. Locos became heavier too: before 1912, few if any orders were for locos of more than 13 tons' weight, the most common were 10-12 tons. From 1920 on, 15 tons became the norm, with some of 20 tons or even more. The heavier weight was apparent in larger boilers and side tanks, both probably a reflection of longer networks and heavier trains.

With growing Japanese domination of supply, all its major manufacturers as well as some smaller ones appear to have supplied Taiwanese mills: at least one loco came from the little known Motoe Machinery Company, for example. But foreign suppliers were not completely excluded; Henschel won orders for both 0-4-0Ts and 0-8-0Ts in 1939 although the outbreak of war appears to have delayed delivery of the 0-8-0Ts at least until 1947. Exceptions apart, however, as the years went by the order books were increasingly dominated by just two suppliers, Nippon Sharyo and Kawasaki.

Although TSC's records show Orenstein & Koppel as the dominant non-Japanese supplier of 0-6-2Ts, O&K's own works records show only three locos of this wheel

Suantou mill in modern times. To the left, two Diema diesels head rakes of sugar wagons converted to carry tourists and to the extreme right is a small inspection trolley. Between the two is TSC no 650, an 0-6-2T with supplementary tender, one of three originally supplied by Orenstein & Koppel to the Meiji sugar company in 1930. This locomotive was restored to working order in 2017.

arrangement supplied, all in 1930 to Dai Nippon. Nor does this wheel arrangement generally appear to have been a common one for O&K. Yet three O&K 0-6-2Ts have survived into preservation, two in Japan and one in Taiwan, none of them seemingly from the 1930 order. The discrepancy is probably explained by trailing wheels being added locally, presumably to improve the stability of the locos, especially if supplementary tenders were also to be used, a not uncommon practice on some lines. Indeed, the 1930 deliveries appear to have been the last steam locomotives O&K supplied to Taiwan, so the 0-6-2 arrangement may well have been specified in the light of experience with earlier 0-6-0Ts or conversions. Among earlier sugar mill locos preserved in Taiwan can be found examples of an 0-8-0T (Kawasaki, 1925) and 0-6-2T+Ts (Nippon Sharyo and O&K) while old photos also show examples of Henschel 0-8-0Ts and at least one Nippon Sharyo 0-6-0 tender loco from 1939.

The increasing trials in the 1930s with ethanol as a fuel or fuel additive did not escape the mill railways. Taiwanese sources record 12 light, two axle petrol locomotives being introduced in Japanese times and used for shunting and several small petrol or petrol-ethanol railcars also made an introduction. As with similar vehicles in other countries, these were of generally low capacity, suitable only for off-peak services or the carriage of mails and their impact appears to have been limited.

By early 1941 all but one of the eight companies active in the sugar industry had a railway system. The network covered just under 2100 route-km with a total fleet of 279 locomotives, to which should be added a small number of railcars. The smallest system was that of the east coast Taitung Sugar Company: just 18.3km long with 3 locomotives. But the largest network, that of the Dai Nippon Sugar Corporation, ran to 666 route-km and a fleet of 76 locomotives. The actual track mileage was considerably greater: the 1938 census recorded the same length of track (2100km) for the 'exclusive use of' sugar companies in Taichung province alone although this also included an unspecified length of push-cart lines owned by the mills.

The post-war years: Nationalisation and modernisation

During the 2nd World War, the Allied Powers had agreed that Taiwan should be given back to China (the Taiwanese were not given any say in the matter) and with the end of hostilities the then Chinese government under Chiang Kai Shek moved quickly to occupy the island. The sugar industry was in a bad way, with equipment worn out or removed for strategic use elsewhere. The production of ethanol from sugar made the mills and refineries military targets and those on the east coast in particular were bombed by the US Air Force. China itself had suffered badly and was about to go into its own civil war culminating in the Communist victory in 1949. But the export earning potential of the sugar industry made it of strategic importance and despite growing road competition, the common carrier lines continued to provide the principal form of public transport for many communities. In 1949, admittedly a somewhat chaotic and therefore perhaps atypical year, the sugar mill lines carried 10% of all rail-passenger traffic in the country, their highest ever proportion. The industry was nationalised, all the mills, their accompanying railways and around one-third of the cane fields being taken over by the Taiwan Sugar Corporation (TSC).

Prior to nationalisation, the different companies had maintained separate railway networks, albeit on the same gauge, using very similar locomotives and working in close geographical proximity. One early consequence of nationalisation was the creation of a unified railway network, joining up the different systems. This led to a continuous, albeit circuitous, alternative railway route from Taichung in the centre of the country all the way to beyond Kaohsiung in the south, creating a network of 2900 route km at maximum extent. The apparent reason for this was to provide an alternative strategic line of communication should China invade and the main railway line be cut. How effective a meandering, single track 762mm gauge railway would have been in such circumstances must be open to question. Most probably the idea arose on a desk in a bureaucracy rather than from on the ground experience and is indicative of the prevalent mood of paranoia in the government at the time.

It certainly did not meet any operational need from the sugar corporation's point of view. The number of common carrier lines did not change and although it meant a locomotive could move all the way from Kaohsiung to Taichung over TSC metals, in practical terms this was hardly necessary or likely. The network was still three times the extent of that of the TRA, scope for rationalisation was limited and this,

TSC no 350 (AFB 2650 of 1948) on static display today at the Xingying mill. 25 July 2016.

plus volume and nature of traffic, justified extensive workshop facilities in several locations. For good measure, the TSC continued to be structured along the lines of the pre-war industry with all the largest mills continuing to be managed independently of one another.

Despite the war years, there had been ongoing investment in the network, reflecting its importance to Japan's wartime economy. The main loco fleet also continued to grow, mainly through local acquisitions – an 0-6-2T built by Taiwan Iron Works in 1941 is among the fleet currently preserved in Taiwan – but the bulk of the existing loco fleet was over 20 years old and had suffered from lack of maintenance during the war. Major overhauls were a priority. As an example, of the 35 locos given major overhauls in 1951, nine had covered over 100,000 kilometres since their last such overhaul and two of them over 150,000km.

Overhauls alone were not enough, however, new motive power was also badly needed. Anti-Japanese feeling in China, if not Taiwan, was high so there was never much prospect of orders going to Japanese builders, even if they had been in any position to supply them at this stage. Taiwanese manufacturers had already supplied some locos pre-war but they were probably not able to deliver on the scale or timetable required. So the new political masters turned to Europe to meet their needs. Some 0-8-0Ts were supplied by Henschel in 1947 (although these may have been an earlier order delayed by the war) but for the bulk of the new fleet they turned to two Belgian manufacturers, Tubize and Anglo-Franco-Belge. Around 45 new locos were delivered, all built in 1948. Twenty-one remain in existence today, 15 of them from Tubize. By this stage and based very much on Japanese experience and practice, standardisation was the order of the day and all the new locos were coal fired 0-6-0 side tanks to very similar designs and specifications.

This was not the first post-war order, however. As mentioned earlier, experiments had already taken place with internal combustion, while an early local effort built on the frames and wheels of a steam locomotive has been preserved at Huwei mill. Building on this experience, 1948 also saw delivery of 15 petrol-engined locos, built by Fate-Root-Heath of the US and fitted with 160hp Plymouth Hercules engines modified to use ethanol (Established in 1910, Fate-Root-Heath was a pioneer in internal combustion railway locomotives but perhaps better known by the Plymouth name carried on its products. The company name changed to Plymouth in the 1950s). The following year delivery was taken of a number of similarly modified petrol-engined railcars to improve passenger services.

As elsewhere, the future was seen to lie with internal combustion. At the time this was not diesel, but either petrol or more usually ethanol, using the capability for producing this that the Japanese had developed. Politics may have been one reason for ethanol's extensive use. Regional tensions remained very high throughout the 1950s following the Korean War and with frequent shelling of Taiwan-controlled Kinmen (Quemoy) by the Chinese. Using ethanol reduced the need for imported fuel and the risk of disruption in its delivery. In contrast to the extensive early use of ethanol there is no evidence that the steam loco fleet ever used anything but coal as fuel, despite the popularity of bagasse for this purpose elsewhere. The Hawaiian-Philippines mill in Negros for example relied entirely on bagasse as loco fuel to the very end of steam working at the end of the 20th century. The early Plymouth locos were followed by 12 of domestic manufacture, using General Motors petrol engines designed for light army trucks. Then in 1956-7, a large order of 50 120hp locos was provided under US aid funds, the locos being built at Brookville in Pennsylvania and equipped with International Harvester engines, also modified to run on ethanol.

The 1950s were the heyday of the network both in extent and in volume of traffic. Between 1952 and 1964 sugar was Taiwan's biggest export earner, at its peak accounting for 80% of all the country's export earnings and the industry employed more than 100,000 people. By 1954, after an intensive programme of overhauls and new deliveries, the total motive power fleet included around 370 steam locomotives although the serviceable number probably did not exceed 350. Barely 20% of the fleet was less than 20 years old, however, and traffic was continuing to grow.

In 1960 the network and operations would still be familiar to someone who had known the lines forty years earlier. Some mills had closed, notably the one at Puli with its 610mm gauge network, which went in 1954, as had some of the lines. But this was mainly through rationalisation or development, not retrenchment. New branch lines of the 1067mm TRA system replaced some of the sugar branch lines while improved interchange facilities made others redundant. But there was also duplication of services. The sugar cane line to Ershui, served by TRA, was still in use in 1969 and in the mid-1960s TSC was running a petrol railcar service between Taichung and Ershui via Nantou, even though TRA offered a much quicker and more direct service. Common carrier services were still offered over almost 600km of track, little changed

Wushulin mill, one of the 1948 Plymouth/Fate-Root-Heath locos on display, 19 May 2007.

from the peak, using either railcars or loco hauled coaches. But their importance as a mode of transport had declined greatly – in 1960 just 2% of rail passengers used sugar mill trains, down from 10% just over a decade earlier.

The future therefore looked promising and with it the requirement for new motive power. Doubts about the suitability of ethanol, or internal combustion more generally, may have started to surface after the large delivery from Brookville as the next order was for steam locos, conventional 0-6-0Ts to the same basic design as the earlier Belgian ones but supplied by the Taiwan Machinery Co. in 1958. This was to be the final order for steam locomotives. Although another 16 locos from different US manufacturers, all fitted with Waukesha petrol engines modified for ethanol, were to be delivered, reservations about ethanol's use also continued to grow. A single loco designed to run on multiple fuel options was bought from Schoema in then West Germany in 1960 but the trials do not appear to have been a success as no further orders followed.

The seasonal nature of sugar production meant that much of the motive power saw use only for a short period each year, so while internal combustion had its advantages, the capital cost of purchasing new motive power had to be set against the likely level of use and retaining the steam locomotive fleet for the traffic peaks of the milling season therefore made sense. The sugar corporation's statistics tell the story. As late as 1964 36 locos from 19 works or sites received heavy overhauls and of these 14 had covered over 100,000km since their last such overhaul. The previous year the

One of four remaining locos supplied by the Skagit Iron and Steel Works in the late 1950s, originally fitted with Waukesha petrol engines. Nominally preserved, it has suffered from being exposed to the elements. Wushulin, 25 July 2016.

respective figures had been 32 and 12 and in 1962, 29 and 11. One of these, 0-6-0T no 317 built by Taiwan Ironworks in 1942, had covered no fewer than 220,000km since its last heavy overhaul.

The public service railcar fleet was generally newer, most of it dating from 1949 or later. But in this too the use of ethanol appears to have been a mixed success at best. So, with sugar exports holding up well and the loco fleet starting to age, the decision was taken in the mid-1960s to start replacing both steam and ethanol by conventional diesel power. As a first step, 54 new 200hp. diesel hydraulic locos were bought from Hitachi in Japan in 1967-9. The previous year, 1966, the original Plymouth ethanol locos of 1948 had been converted to diesel traction, using considerably more powerful 385hp. Allis Chalmers engines. This enabled almost all the remaining pre-war fleet of steam locomotives to be withdrawn from service.

By the 1970s Taiwan's success as one of the first Asian 'Tiger economies' was feeding through to ordinary people in increased prosperity and rising living standards. The common carrier services fell victim to this, as traffic declined rapidly and they became increasingly uneconomic. The number of lines on which such services were offered fell from a peak of 41 to 17 by 1971. Although they still covered almost 400km of route, by this time services were almost certainly being run at the direct request of the government, whether or not in return for a subsidy is not clear. But the industry

One of the working TSC steam locos – and the only one coal-fired – is no 346, AFB 2654 of 1948, based at Xihu mill where it heads regular tourist trains. It is seen here at the mill alongside TSC 837, a Hitachi loco from 1967, also used to haul tourist trains. 15 November 2008.

The works plate on TSC 346.

A preserved staff railcar in use at Suantou mill, 22 September 2006. Although still at the mill, it is no longer in working order.

overall remained in a healthy state. Although its importance as an export earner was in steady decline with the rise of the textile and electronics industries, in 1976 25 sugar mills remained in production and the TSC rail network was still over 2000km in total length.

In a vote of confidence in the future, the sugar corporation's management decided first to re-engine all the remaining ethanol powered locos (mainly the 'Brookville' fleet of the mid-1950s) and then on a further major order of new motive power. In 1973 Japan established diplomatic relations with Mao Zedong's People's Republic of China, switching recognition from the rival Republic of China of Chiang Kai-shek on Taiwan. In retaliation, the government in Taipei imposed a boycott of Japanese products, so the sugar corporation turned to Diema of Germany to meet its requirements, first for 66 new locomotives in 1977, then a further 25 in 1979, the first batch with Mercedes engines, the second with Allis-Chalmers but both of 247 hp. As with the earlier Hitachi deliveries, these were 0-6-0 diesel hydraulics. Only with delivery of the second batch did regular steam working finally come to an end. Although this had been in steady decline for some years, steam power could still be seen on passenger trains as late as 1978, its final regular use coming in the 1979 sugar milling season.

Retrenchment and re-direction

Apart from three more Hitachi locos for use on 1067mm gauge track and ordered after the boycott on Japanese products had been lifted, the Diemas were to be the last new locos ordered by the TSC. Their delivery was to prove the high-water mark for the sugar industry in Taiwan. World sugar prices collapsed after 1976, domestic costs were simultaneously rising and common carrier traffic had all but collapsed as passengers deserted trains for their own motor-scooters on the newly built roads. By 1979 services were still offered over only 120km of track but even this level was not sustainable. The last remaining passenger trains, over the 19km between Chiayi and Beigang to the west, were finally withdrawn in 1981. Their withdrawal also saw the end of Chiayi station's status of offering services of three different companies on two separate gauges, the other providers being the TRA and the Forestry Bureau on the Alishan railway.

The rapid changes in Taiwan's economy meant that the sugar industry no longer held the strategic importance it had two decades previously. Many of the mills, state of the art when first opened, were now relatively small and inefficient by world standards, or were more easily served by trucks on improving roads. As Taiwan's population grew, so land devoted to sugar production could increasingly be put to more productive use. Of 25 mills still working in the mid-1970s, most of them relying on railways to deliver cane from the fields, fewer than half were still in production by the turn of the century and the rail network was down to just 240km, less than 10% of its peak. Today Taiwan Sugar Corporation has just two working sugar mills and one refinery.

That is not the end of the story. First, one of the two surviving mills, at Huwei in Yunlin County, the heartland of sugar production north-west of Chiayi, is still served by rail. The operations here at the height of the milling season are in marked contrast to those in better known sugar cane countries, with an intensity rare anywhere on the narrow gauge today. Light tracks into the fields themselves have long gone. Instead, initial loading of cut cane is into tipper trucks which then transfer the cane into high capacity rail wagons at specially built loading ramps. The track into the mill is laid to a high standard for an industrial line (the TSC even acquired a Plasser & Theurer tamper in the mid-1980s!) and bright yellow Diema diesel hydraulics bring in long rakes of loaded wagons at frequent intervals throughout the day. Unloading through a wagon tippler is fast while a large marshalling yard and radio controlled operations help support 24/7 working and quick turnarounds. In common with some other mills, until quite recently Huwei was also served by a 1067mm gauge line. 762mm gauge trains brought cane to the mill for refining and 1067mm gauge trains took the refined product to exchange sidings for handing over to TRA. One result was an extensive network of dual-gauge track, including some complicated point work, which remains *in situ*.

Second, closure of the mills coincided with a growing interest in Taiwan in its industrial heritage and the rise of a domestic leisure movement. This has helped ensure the survival of no fewer than 45 of TSC's former steam fleet, about half of them being post-war deliveries. Most are now on static display at a variety of locations around the island but some have gone to Japan while at least two are in working order and still see use in Taiwan at the old mills at Wushulin and Xihu. Although the TSC

Following nationalisation in 1945, the Sugar Corporation embarked on a major new investment programme. This included an upgrading of passenger trains, in connection with which 2 petrol-electric railcars were ordered from Hitachi in 1949. No 538, seen here, saw almost thirty years of service from 1950 until withdrawal in 1979. It is today preserved at Wushulin. 25 July 2016.

sold one of its surplus Diemas to the Welshpool & Llanfair Railway in the UK in 2004, where it will be familiar to many UK enthusiasts, and another to a French private railway the following year, these were exceptions. With large numbers of surplus diesel locomotives and cane cars and few prospective buyers, the TSC decided to put many of them to work on tourist trains, often with the support of local councils. Most of these are occasional workings, often to coincide with local festivals or events, along short lengths of surviving track, with brightly painted locos hauling short trains of equally garish but rudimentary carriages converted from cane cars and aimed firmly at the family afternoon fun market.

The policy was also aimed at retaining jobs for an ageing workforce who would otherwise find new opportunities difficult if not impossible to find and with this in mind, the mills at Suantou and Xihu have been preserved as industrial museums, complete with short stretches of working railway, while that at Wushulin has been turned into a museum of the sugar cane railways with preserved railcars, inspection vehicles and diesel locos also on display. As noted above, both Wushulin and Xihu have a working steam locomotive. That at Xihu is TSC no 346, an Anglo-Franco-Belge product, works no 2654, which sees regular use at weekends and holidays. Wushulin's loco is also from the 1948 Belgian order, in this case a Tubize, works no 2354, TSC no 370.

Four former mills currently offer regular tourist services, usually using Diema diesels, as in this picture of no 150 at Xingying mill on 25 July 2016. Note the mixed gauge pointwork in the foreground.

Both were originally plinthed before being restored to working order but while Xihu's remains coal-fired, the Tubize at Wushulin has been converted to oil-firing, allowing a single person to operate it with ease. At least one other post war 0-6-0T is preserved in working order in Japan.

All three mills have proved popular with tourists. Recently, however, TSC appears to have been having further thoughts about the long-term viability of them as museums or attractions. As older employees retire, they are not being replaced, so the skills necessary to keep locomotives in running order are gradually disappearing. One consequence is that the Tubize at Wushulin is no longer steamed regularly, being restricted at the time of writing (2016) to special occasions or for charters. Two railcars at Suantou which were previously available for charters are also now out of commission. More generally and even more worryingly, TSC appears increasingly reluctant to commit resources to maintaining the facilities in good order. Suantou mill was badly damaged in typhoons around 2010, since when it has been closed to visitors although the railway remains open. But in 2016 this too shows worrying signs of a lack of attention, with track increasingly overgrown and historic rolling stock slowly rusting away in the yard although the trains are often busier than ever. It is to be hoped that an agreement can be reached between all interested parties to ensure that at least the most significant pieces in TSC's rich and varied collection of historic items will be preserved for the benefit of future generations.

3

HIGHEST AND HARDEST* –
ALISHAN, THE LINE OF THE SHAYS

Forests covered 80% of the Taiwan land mass in the early years of the 20th century. They were of fundamental importance to the aboriginal inhabitants but the Chinese had also recognised at an early stage the importance of forests for environmental reasons – slowing the rate of water run-off and therefore preventing flooding after typhoons, helping stabilise land to reduce landslides and providing shelter for agriculture, as well as providing a source of timber, principally camphor wood. The Japanese held similar views but also saw more commercial potential. At the time they first occupied Taiwan they had already built the first logging railway in the Imperial Forest at Kiso, not far from Nagoya.

They approached the exploitation of Taiwan's considerable timber resources in the same methodical way they developed the sugar industry. At an early stage three principal forestry areas were identified: Pahsienshan in the central western mountains, nowadays falling within the administrative district of Taichung City, Taipingshan in the island's north-east and Alishan, the most southerly of the three, lying astride the Tropic of Cancer close to Chiayi City. In due course, all three forest areas were to be linked to the outside world by rail. Of the three, without any doubt the best known to enthusiasts is the line to Alishan.

Until completion earlier this century of the railway to Lhasa in Tibet, this remarkable railway was the highest in Asia, at one time climbing to a summit 2682 metres above sea level at Shishan. It reached this height in a little over 80km from the lower terminus at Chiayi, which stands just 30 metres above sea level. Most of the climbing, some 2100 metres, was done in under 60km and achieved entirely on a conventional, adhesion worked line with no recourse to rack or other forms of assistance. In this the line stands comparison with the better-known lines of the Andes in Peru and Ecuador which achieved similar feats by similar methods: a combination of steep gradients – 5% for much of the line but including stretches at 6% and a peak of 6.55% just before Alishan – tight curves, 50 tunnels, the longest over one kilometre in length, 120 bridges and a series of zig-zags or switchbacks on the final approach to Alishan.

Capping all this is an outstanding, possibly unique, piece of engineering at Dulishan, shortly after the line starts to climb in earnest. Taiwanese mountains have nothing in common with the gentle rolling downs of England or even the more rugged slopes of the Scottish Highlands. They are immediately familiar to anyone who has studied oriental brush paintings, with seemingly impossibly vertiginous slopes rising

---

*   With acknowledgements to Brian Fawcett who to my knowledge was the first to use this phrase, to describe the Central Railway of Peru in his superb book *Railways of the Andes*. But it seems an equally appropriate description of the Alishan line.

A classic early view of Shay no 15 with a loaded train. The position of the locomotive, with the smokebox next to the train, reveals this to be on the Dadajia branch, which retained many of its timber trestle viaducts to the very end of services in the 1970s.

National Central Library of Taiwan

A downhill train crossing trestle no 91 behind Shay no 23, March 1966. Since then all the viaducts have been rebuilt using either steel or concrete girders.

M Umemura

In steam days Fenchihu, 45km from Chiayi, was the loco changeover and division point. 28 ton Shays nos. 31 and 32 (Lima 2946 and 2947 respectively of 1917), the last two supplied to the line await their next turns of duty, March 1966. At least one more locomotive can be seen in the shed behind. Today it is a museum. No 31 remains in service today, based at Alishan shed, but has been converted to oil-firing.

M Umemura

steeply from valleys below. The engineers came face to face with this mountain wall at Dulishan. In contrast to the similar situation at Alishan itself, however, which left no alternative to resorting to switchbacks, at Dulishan the geology had created an isolated peak standing alone from the main mountain range but connected to it by a narrow ridge. Around this mountain the engineers tunnelled out a triple spiral culminating in a figure of eight, through which the line gained sufficient height to then run along the connecting ridge and thereby gain access to the mountain wall. Local legend has it that the layout was inspired by the spiral rings and conical shape of a snail shell.

As the eagles fly, Jhangnaoliao at the foot of the mountain wall and Liyuanlin, the next station but one up the line are just 2km apart but at a difference of 360 metres in height. The railway covers 8.1km to join the two, on a near constant grade of 5%, lessening only through the station at Dulishan itself. This section in particular must have been a surveyor's nightmare, even trying to follow the route on a map is a challenge!

The best engineering comparison is probably the Bergün spirals on the Rhaetian railway in Switzerland, completed just a few years earlier, where the line to St Moritz takes 12km to gain 417 metres of height and 6.5km on the ground. As Charles Small

The essence of the Alishan railway but rarely seen by visitors. In this 1972 scene Shay no 17 (Lima 2634 of 1913) prepares to leave Dadajia with a loaded train. The log loading tackle is clearly visible behind the train.
Kurashige Nobutaka

put it in *Rails to the Setting Sun*: *Certainly no other timber line in the world was so carefully engineered and probably no other timber line was so expensive.*

The Japanese were clearly not averse to spending large sums of money on logging lines, for Small separately noted that they spent the then considerable sum of $125,000/mile on rebuilding the Kiso Forest Railway for steam traction in the second decade of the 20th century. In the case of the Alishan line, however, they may well have had other motives for the expense apart from timber extraction alone for a 1910 survey of Taiwan's forests noted that:

> *The district where the greater part of the State forests in Formosa [Taiwan] lies, is inhabited by the barbarians who have not been brought under the civilizing influence and frequently they inflict damages upon the people crossing the boundary lines. Until these barbarians are tamed and made good citizens of the Empire, the utilization of these forests … is next to impossible.*[*]

A well-engineered railway would not only allow logs to be brought down but would open up a large area of the central mountains to speedy access by police and troops, allowing much more effective action against the aboriginal tribes who still controlled

---

[*]   Bureau of Forestry report, Department of Agriculture & Commerce, Tokyo 1910.

Loading complete, no 17 descends towards Alishan with the train seen in the previous photo. The way the line was built on the edge of the mountain can be clearly seen in this photo.

Kurashige Nobutaka

Nos 17 and 18 were two of the last two cylinder Shays to remain in service, surviving almost to the very end of steam working and ending their days on station pilot duties at Alishan. They are here seen on shed at Alishan in 1972.

Kurashige Nobutaka

most of the mountain areas. From the very beginning, the railway offered passenger and goods services as far as Alishan, in addition to its core business of bringing down logs from the mountains. Most of these were felled in areas beyond Alishan itself, a series of branch lines being built further into the mountains for this purpose.

Although government backing for building the railway was given in 1903, financial constraints due to the war with Russia meant that work only started in 1906, initially under private enterprise in the form of the Fujita Group. The first 14km from Chiayi to Jhuci across the plains were completed without difficulty and by October 1907 the spirals at Dulishan had been completed when it became apparent that construction of the line as far as Alishan would be beyond the resources of private enterprise. The Japanese Government stepped in, handing over responsibility for the line to its Forestry Bureau. The line reached Erwanping in December 1912 and Alishan four months later. Local services appear to have been provided between Chiayi and Jhuci almost from the beginning but passenger and general freight traffic to and from Alishan did not start until 1920.

Between Jhuci and Alishan intermediate sources of traffic were few, with the notable exception of Jhangnaoliao (樟腦寮) at the bottom of the Dulishan spiral. This was an important area for camphor trees (the name translates literally as 'camphor wood hut') so extra sidings were laid in anticipation of the traffic. But the steeply sloping hillside did not allow the construction of a conventional station layout so the station

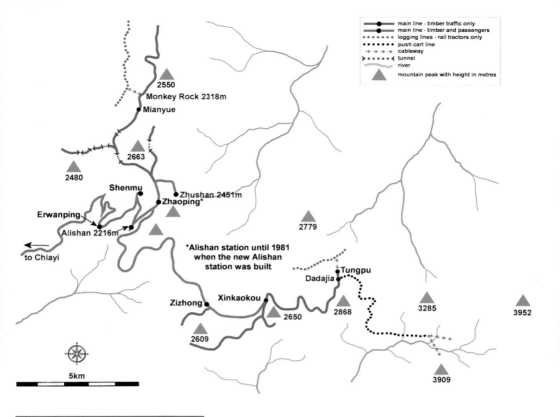

The railway network around Alishan.

John Athersuch

and its sidings were built into the hill on a terrace above the line of railway, which rose steeply from the Jhuci direction to the station throat. Ascending trains would therefore have to pass the station and reverse in. This layout had three advantages. First, wagons could be stationed on the level while they were being loaded, second, ascending trains which had stopped at the station would be able to re-start on the level rather than a 5% grade and finally the station sidings could double as escape lines for any runaway train coming down the spiral, assuming it could negotiate the spiral's tight curves without mishap.

Beyond Jhangnaoliao, it was not until the approaches to Alishan itself that the real prize in traffic terms became accessible. This was the extensive forests of *hinoki,* or red cypress and spruce. The former was especially prized for use in Shinto temples, Alishan timber being used in Tokyo's Yakusuni shrine. Logging soon started in earnest. As it did so, so new lines were built beyond Alishan further into the mountains to exploit the resources. To begin with two lines were built, roughly north-west and south-east from Alishan, following the ridge line and being extended in stages as the timber sources were logged out (from the outset the Japanese maintained a conservative policy of felling and re-planting but with some of the most valuable timber coming from trees some hundreds of years old, the demand for new sources of old growth timber was near-constant). Although these were technically branch lines, and most of the ascent was on the 'main' line up to Alishan, there was no question of them being secondary in

Shay no 12 on shed at Alishan, September 1974. Following an early accident some of the first Shays were re-numbered and as Lima works no 2351 of 1910, no 12 was in fact the very first Shay delivered to the line and together with sisters 17 and 18 officially remained in service until the end of steam in November 1984.

John Tillman

engineering terms. The conflicted nature of Taiwan's mountains still required extensive use of trestle viaducts, tunnels and avalanche shelters as the lines extended further into the mountains. The southern, or Tungpu branch would keep its timber trestles until the very end of its working life in 1978. Much of its track bed now forms a road leading towards Yushan or Jade Mountain, Taiwan's highest peak. On the northern, or Mianyue branch, many of the avalanche shelters and viaducts were replaced over time by concrete structures. As logging ended in the 1980s, this line saw growing tourist traffic before being put out of commission by severe damage in a 1999 earthquake.

Eventually these two branch lines, together with shorter spurs, would be almost as long in combined length as the main line from Chiayi to Alishan, effectively doubling the length of the system to about 150km. By the 1920s the full potential of Taiwan's forests had become clear and the Japanese were keen to exploit it to the full. But as logging extended further from Alishan, so there were limits as to how far lines could be built in such a grand style. Taiwan's mountains are formed principally of one long continuous ridge from north to south from which precipitous valleys fall away on either side. The two branch lines and the shorter spurs had therefore penetrated the mountains to the maximum extent practical. Any new railway line to gain access to timber stands on adjacent mountains would have to start again from the valley floor at ruinous expense. The answer to this problem lay in a series of aerial ropeways from locations on the branches to adjacent mountains.

Dulishan spiral. A rare view showing three levels of the Dulishan spiral, with a train on the second level. When it reaches the level above, it will be travelling in the opposite direction and will have yet one more level to traverse before reaching the top of the spiral. Today this view is almost obscured by trees.

Su Chao Hsu

But a way still had to be found to bring out the timber to the ropeways. Conventional locomotives would have been far too heavy to be taken over the ropeways, so both railways and rolling stock would have to be as lightly constructed as possible. The challenge was to find locos that were lighter than the smaller Shays, yet capable of performing on very lightly laid track, while also reducing the ever-present risk of forest fires from steam locomotives. The solution lay in small loco-tractors, not unlike the early Simplex locos then growing in popularity in the UK. The Forestry Bureau was already undertaking trials of similar tractors on the Kiso Forest Railway in Japan, where the Kato company of Tokyo had started making petrol-engined locos and railcars in 1923. It was designated the supplier of them to the Japanese Ministry of Railways the same year.

In 1926 two short wheel-base, 7 ton industrial locos from Kato fitted with Whitcomb engines from the USA arrived. They were only a little more than one-third the weight of the smaller Shays, so capable of operating over much lighter track. Powered by charcoal gas, they appear to have been an immediate success and were quickly followed by a larger number of similar locos from the Kato works but this time with Japanese made engines. Although charcoal gas may seem an odd fuel it was common during the Second World War due to fuel shortages and was attractive in Taiwan for the same reason. Petrol had to be imported and was expensive while the raw material for the gas was in abundant local supply. Its main disadvantage was the

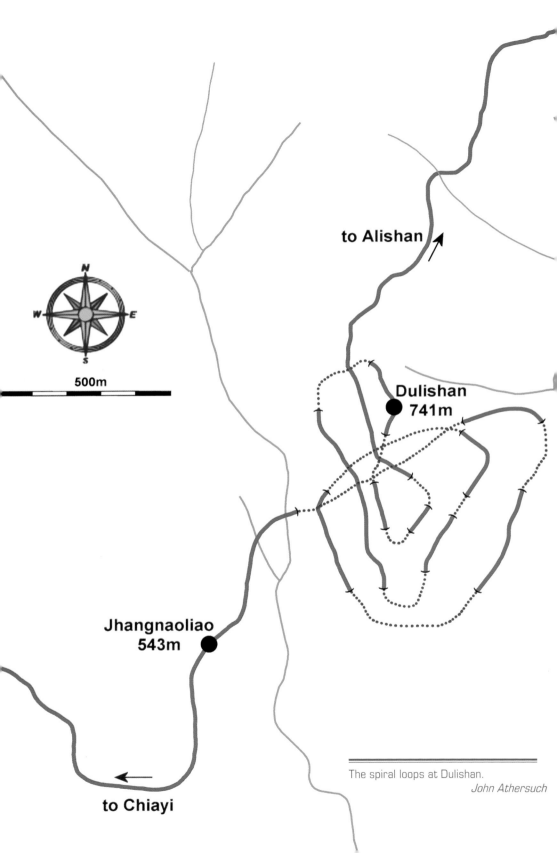

N

W   E

S

500m

to Alishan

Dulishan
741m

Jhangnaoliao
543m

to Chiayi

The spiral loops at Dulishan.
John Athersuch

need for a very large tank for the gas, less of an issue on logging lines where locos were covering relatively short distances and often stationary for much of the time so did not need to carry such extensive fuel reserves. The tractors at Alishan all seem to have been converted to either petrol or diesel fuel as soon as fuel supplies became easier after the second war but charcoal gas was used as a fuel on some other Taiwanese logging lines into the 1950s.

The success of the early tractors paved the way for construction of further lines of between 4 and 8km in length on adjacent mountain sides, built out from aerial ropeways, thereby opening up significant new areas of forest. In due course Kato came up with a series of such locomotives, all of similar design but from 4 to 7 tons in weight to take account of different circumstances. Together with similar locomotives from American manufacturers, these allowed the economical exploitation of the other forest reserves in Taiwan as will be explained in subsequent chapters. In contrast to the heavy engineering of the Alishan line, the lines in these reserves were much more lightly engineered throughout and made much more extensive use of ropeways to minimise construction costs. In much the same way that push-cart lines opened the way to wider economic development of the island, so the advent of reliable, small internal combustion loco tractors enabled the full exploitation of the island's extensive timber resources.

Although Alishan was primarily a timber town, the Japanese also started to develop it as a tourist resort, planting cherry trees and laying out parks and woodland trails. Its altitude proved especially welcoming in the summer months when the cooler air provided a welcome respite from the heat and humidity of the plains. Nearby Yushan (Niikatayama to the Japanese) was the highest mountain in the Japanese Empire, surpassing Mt Fuji and therefore a popular hiking destination. Completion of the south-easterly Tungpu branch shortened the hike considerably and passenger services were provided to meet the demand. But passenger services were always secondary to the main business of bringing down timber. Timetabled passenger services only started in 1920 and over the mainline there were never more than two or three passenger trains daily. The 1940 timetable for example shows two trains in each direction between Chiayi and Alishan, with one continuing to and starting from Xinkaokou. Between Chiayi and Jhuci, however, with villages and local traffic to tap, services were more frequent with six round trips. Although school services continued to be provided into the 1970s the rise of road competition saw all these local services ended by 1980.

Sixty years after opening the basic service remained two daily workings although there have been regular experiments over the years in response to either growing traffic volumes or competition. In 1946 275,000 passengers were carried. This dropped to 188,000 in 1950 in the chaos following the Chinese occupation but recovered to reach 372,000 in 1960. Until the 1980s restrictions on passports and exchange controls made overseas travel difficult if not impossible, so domestic tourism also grew steadily from the 1950s. Demand for tickets to Alishan regularly exceeded supply, especially at peak periods and in response the first diesel railcars were introduced, although the basic timetable does not appear to have been changed.

In the mid-1980s, following the completion of a road to Alishan, there was a step change in the standard of passenger accommodation with the introduction of new, air-conditioned carriages with panoramic windows and reclining seats. With their

Weekend traffic at Dulishan station. The vicinity is a popular hiking area and despite the provision of additional services, there is frequently standing room only on trains at peak periods. 19 November 2016.

advent, an overnight service was also introduced. This left Chiayi at 01.00 in the morning, arriving at Alishan at 04.00. The downhill return was in daylight hours and the service was aimed clearly at the growing number of visitors wishing to see the sunrise over Yushan, especially those with limited time available. But it was not a success and by 1988 the timetable had reverted to two round trips daily, falling to just one from 1990.

In retrospect, the 1970s could be considered the heyday of the Alishan line. Freight tonnage had fully recovered from the chaos and uncertainty of the post-war years, peaking in 1958 at 102,000 tons. Thereafter it started to decline but timber was still being brought down the mountain while the growth in tourism made the line busier than ever, especially as the railway was the only means of access to Alishan and the high mountains around. Although starting to be replaced, the original steam locomotives remained very much in use, especially on the branch lines above Alishan, if less so on the main line. The 1980s were to bring major change. In 1982 a road was opened to Alishan leading to an inevitable and immediate decline in tourist rail traffic. Timber traffic was already in decline and by the end of the decade the government had implemented a total ban on logging in the national forest areas for environmental reasons. Steam traction finally came to a formal end in November 1984. Six Shays notionally remained in working order although the boiler certificates of at least two, maybe more, had in fact expired. In practice remaining use had already been confined to Alishan station pilot duties for at least the previous two years, two locomotives normally being more than sufficient for this.

DL25, built by Mitsubishi in 1969 and the prototype for the successful diesel design for the line, still in service almost forty years later, on an early morning shuttle for sunrise viewing at Zhushan, 16 July 2007.

But the railway remains very much a going concern. Tourists may no longer depend on the railway to reach Alishan but they visit the resort in greater numbers than ever, especially since large numbers of Chinese tourists started coming to Taiwan in recent years. The railway has adapted accordingly. One of the most popular activities is to rise early to see the sunrise over Yushan, or Jade Mountain, the highest peak in Taiwan (and the old Japanese Empire) at 3952 metres. Since 1986, to reach the viewing area from Alishan they have had two options, either a long hike up the mountain in the pre-dawn cold and dark, or a short ride on a train up one of the former logging branches to Zhushan station, 6.25km away and at 2451 metres above sea level, 235 metres higher than Alishan itself. Not surprisingly, most tourists take the train! So, in the hours between 0400 and 0600 the railway operates an intensive shuttle service over this stretch. Even so, on many trains it is 'standing room only.' With bench seating down either side of the carriage, pitch darkness outside and the roar of the diesel on the 6% grade, the experience must be reminiscent of conditions on the very earliest London tube line back in 1890. This service alone carries around 40% of all the line's passengers with another 40% carried on short day time shuttle services between Alishan and Zhaoping and Shenmu. Passenger revenue covers 95% of the operating costs of these trains, the balance being covered by the entrance fee to the National Park. By contrast, fares cover only 50% of the operating costs of trains on the 'main' line. A large new station building has been recently completed at Alishan to cope with this new traffic and the railway now carries around 1.4 million passengers annually.

Empty coaching stock in the pre-dawn light at Zhushan station awaiting passengers returning from viewing the sunrise over Jade Mountain, 5 May 2016.

Keeping the line open is both a challenging and very expensive business. A 1999 earthquake destroyed the old Mianyue logging branch to Shihou, or Monkey Rock, which until then had seen a nascent tourist operation developing. The impact of Typhoon Morakot in 2009 was even more disastrous. Landslides caused by the typhoon washed away much of the main line. Full repairs were estimated in the high tens of millions of dollars but academics warned that even after repair the geology of the area meant that the line would remain susceptible to damage in future typhoons or earthquakes. Partial abandonment and replacement by a cableway was considered before the government finally decided to press ahead with full reconstruction. At the time of writing the railway still has not been fully re-opened, main line operations being confined to the section between Chiayi and the old sub-division point at Fenchihu, roughly halfway to Alishan. Full re-opening to Alishan requires the complete rebuilding of tunnel no. 46, the longest on the line at over 1.1km and is not expected before 2019.

Further controversy surrounded a 2008 decision to transfer operation of the railway to the private sector. In an issue reminiscent of the transfer of the line from the private sector to the Japanese Government just over a century earlier, the Forestry Bureau took back operation of the railway in 2010, claiming the private operator had failed to achieve agreed operating and repair targets. In 2011 the Forestry Bureau transferred management responsibility to the Taiwan Railways Administration (TRA) which has embarked on a major drive to promote the railway, including signing a 'sister railway' agreement with Switzerland's Matterhorn Gotthard Bahn, which adds to ones signed previously with Japanese lines.

Three of the Alishan railway's Shays remain in working order, two of them, nos 25 and 31 converted to oil firing. For a period in 2007 and 2008 the railway ran regular weekend steam trains between Chiayi and Jhuci using no 25, which is normally kept at Chiayi's Beimen depot. Here 25 awaits departure with the afternoon return working from Jhuci, 4 August 2007.

Despite rebuilding and modernisation, including computer assisted controls, maintenance of the Shays remains a labour intensive exercise. A midway stop provides an opportunity for lubrication, 4 August 2007.

Motive power

While Alishan is famous for its engineering, it is probably even better known for its motive power for the first seventy years or so of its operations, geared Shay locomotives from the USA. For initial construction, however, the contractors used two 27.5 ton 0-8-0Ts built by HK Porter plus a 13 ton 2-cylinder Shay, works no 2001 of 1907. All three locos were transferred back to Japan, the Shay seeing more years of service on the Tsugaru Imperial Forestry railway there. These were initially replaced by a number of conventional 0-6-0Ts from three different suppliers in three different countries: Vulcan Iron Works of the USA, Andrew Barclay of the UK and Kawasaki of Japan. Japanese sources state that the two Barclays were built in 1911. Taiwanese author Su Chao Hsu disputes this, arguing that the two locos were officially nos. 1 and 2 in the railway's numbering and that as initial operations had already started in 1910, the locomotives must have been delivered by this time. The Japanese records list the locomotives as Barclays works numbers 1251 and 1252 of September 1911, which is consistent with other available information, so if Barclay locos were in action before this, they were presumably borrowed from one or more of the sugar mill lines also being built at the time.

There is also some debate about the provenance of the Vulcan tanks. Although they are reported to have been delivered in 1910, the numbering sequence suggests a later date. Small stated that they were bought for the line at the outset but Su gives a different view, claiming that the locomotives were always intended for the east coast railway (see Chapter 5) but on arrival in Taiwan in 1910 three were loaned to the Alishan railway until the latter was able to acquire its own motive power. As the Vulcans were not listed in the official Alishan numbering this is plausible. What is also clear is that the Vulcans went to the east coast line once the first Shays were delivered, while the other locos went to other forestry lines. The Japanese 0-6-0T did not arrive until 1914. Built by Kawasaki as works number 126, at 21 tons weight this was noticeably larger than the other 0-6-0Ts, all of which were of around 15 tons. It appears to have been acquired as a replacement for the Vulcans when they returned to the east coast, specifically for shunting and short trip workings on the flat around Chiayi.

At the same time as ordering the Barclays, the Forestry Bureau ordered eight 18 ton 2 cylinder Shays from Lima. The first two, locos no 11 and 12, Lima works nos. 2351 and 2352 respectively, were delivered in August 1910, in time for the start of operations over the whole line. The remaining six were delivered in batches until 1913 although the first of these, Lima works number 2474, was wrecked in a crash only a few months after arriving. The three remaining 0-6-0Ts were kept for operations in the Chiayi area until loco no 1 (Barclay works no. 1251) was transferred to the Lotung line in 1933 (see Chapter 4) where it became no. 5. Barclay no 2 remained in Chiayi as a yard shunter until 1951 when it too was transferred to Lotung as loco no 14. While many locomotives have survived in Taiwan on static display, unfortunately neither of the Barclays is among them.[*]

---

[*] Su Chao Hsu states that loco no 6 was transferred to Lotung at the same time to become loco no 6 there. But Okita says that Lotung no 6 was a much smaller loco, only 13 tons' weight rather than the 21 tons of Alishan no 6. He too lists it as built by Kawasaki but does not give a works number. Three Andrew Barclay locos were exported to Taiwan in 1910 but the only locos shipped around this time with specifications matching those in Taiwan records for the Alishan ones were works nos. 1251 and 1252, shipped to Taipei in September 1911.

Shay no 25 in steam in Chiayi yard, showing clearly the large W shaped sandbox on the rear of the tender, 4 May 2016.

The Shays must have quickly demonstrated their capabilities but also their limitations, for even before most of the 18 tonners had been delivered, the first of a larger, 28 ton three-cylinder class was delivered in 1912 (works no 2557), to be followed by a further 11 in the succeeding years to 1917. By 1920 therefore the line had a fleet of 19 Shays of two classes. In some respects, they were an odd choice. Despite its narrow gauge, steep gradients and sharp curves, the Alishan line was designed and engineered to much higher standards than was the norm on logging lines. From the outset, operating policy was for the locomotive always to be at the downward end of the train, presumably to reduce the risk of runaways or wagons breaking loose on the steep gradients. This meant forward visibility for crews working uphill was zero, especially on the larger Shays which had full height coal bunkers and they were reliant on bell signalling from a brakeman at the front of the train, while the wholly enclosed cab made for hot and unpleasant working conditions. In circumstances like these more conventional articulated locomotives, Mallets for example, may have been more suitable. On the other hand, the working arrangements did mean the chimney was behind the crew as they worked the trains uphill, no small consideration in the frequent tunnels, while the Shays' geared wheel arrangement presumably provided better adhesion on the grades.

A QUESTION OF NUMBERS – 1

There has been some debate among railway historians on both sides of the Pacific in recent years surrounding the correct builder's number for each Alishan Shay. This arose primarily because of the early wreck of Lima no 2474, originally Alishan no 13. It was assumed that the next delivery, Lima 2549, became no 13 in its place. Taiwan historian Hung Chih-wen has shown however that Lima 2549 became Alishan 14 (now at the Puffing Billy Railway in Australia) while the first two locos were re-numbered, so the line kept a no 13 but lost a no 11. Which of the first two (Lima 2351 and 2352) is now no 12 and which no 13 appears to be lost in the sands of time.

On a Shay locomotive, the cylinders are situated approximately midway along the frame and connected via a crankshaft to driveshafts in each direction. Bevel gears on each driveshaft power each axle through interconnecting gears on the wheels. Alishan railway lore has it a standard Shay locomotive would have twin bevel gears linking each driving wheel whereas the Alishan locomotives only have one, to allow the bogies to turn freely on the line's sharp curves. Larger Shays, for example the former Western Maryland no. 6, now in service on West Virginia's Cass Scenic Railroad, do indeed have twin bevel gears. But drawings in the original Lima catalogues show that single bevel gears were not uncommon, at least on two-truck locomotives. The trucks (or bogies) on the Alishan Shays are also mounted on roller-bearings, similarly to help deal with the curves although whether this was an original feature is not clear. Another feature of the Alishan locos is more immediately noticeable. In line with other Shays, a large sand dome atop the boiler feeds sanders on the front truck. Added to this, however, is a large sandbox behind the bunker to provide sand to the rear truck, in practice the front one on an ascending train. With modifications like these added to the already robust design and relative simplicity of operation, the Shays proved to be ideal for conditions on the Alishan line. They were to be the mainstay of operations for the next fifty years and the last Shays in commercial service anywhere.

Notwithstanding their success, internal combustion power came to Alishan at an early date. As we have already seen, the first loco-tractors were introduced in 1926. By 1950 there were seven in service, all of 7 tons' weight, four diesel-powered and three petrol, the original charcoal gas tractors having been rebuilt after the war. Around the same time the fleet was fitted with air brakes, requiring a pair of distinctive air drums on the cab roof and allowing heavier trains to be hauled. In this form, they proved even more successful, light yet powerful and flexible and the Alishan fleet eventually grew to 27 such locomotives by 1970. Thereafter their use declined along with the reduction in logging but the last of them survived in service until 1994, while later versions of the same basic design could be seen in service on other industrial narrow gauge lines in Taiwan until the very end of the century.

The first trials of non-steam power on the main line also came early, in the form of two 22 seat petrol electric railcars introduced in 1933, presumably with nascent tourist traffic in mind. While they should have offered a quicker and cleaner journey for passengers they do not appear to have been successful and were converted to conventional carriages by the end of the 1940s.

The brake operator's view from a train leaving Alishan station. The steep descent towards Shenmu and Chiayi on the left-hand line is immediately apparent. Note the flagman in addition to colour light signals. 4 May 2016.

A returning 'sunrise' train negotiates the S bends between Zhaoping and Alishan on its descent to the latter, 5 May 2016.

Fenchihu station, the division point between Chiayi and Alishan in steam days and the current limit of mainline operations pending major repairs, on 5 May 2016. The daily train from Chiayi has just arrived, powered by DL49, the most recent addition to the loco fleet.

Not until the early 1950s was further thought given to diesel traction on the main line, possibly spurred by the success of diesel loco-tractors on the logging branches. By this time most of the Shays had also been in service for forty years and must have been showing their age. In 1953 two 25 ton, 225hp diesels arrived on the line from Mitsubishi in Japan. They were diesel-mechanical 0-6-0s to a then new industrial design with a short wheelbase and a significant overhang at either end. The rigid wheelbase and fixed drive to all wheels soon caused problems, especially on tight curves where the difference in radius between the inside and outside rails led to inner wheel slip. They were fitted with large dampers to try to reduce this but other problems remained, notably with the clutch on the mechanical drive, as the friction when starting trains on the grade led both to frequent stalling and excessive clutch plate wear. They were soon confined to school services on the relatively level and straight line between Chiayi and Jhuci and shunting the Chiayi yards, until withdrawn from service in 1970.

It was clear that something more akin to the Shays was needed to cope with the operating conditions so the next tender placed due emphasis on weight, horsepower and a short wheelbase. The first prototypes had been a learning experience for

Together with other logging lines on the island, the lightly laid tramways in the high mountains at Alishan were the preserve of Kato internal combustion locos. Re-engined, most of them proved to be long lived, remaining in service until the end of logging operations. One remains on display in Chiayi's Beimen yard, together with an early example of passenger rolling stock. 4 May 2016.

Mitsubishi too, and the following year they duly obliged with the first of two 25 ton B'B' diesel locos with a hydraulic clutch mechanism. Slightly more powerful than the original two, at 258hp, the design appears to have been a conscious effort to replicate the success of the Shays and avoid the limitations inherent in the rigid wheelbase of the previous diesels. The two bogies with coupled wheels mimicked the arrangement on the Shays, overcame the drawback of a rigid wheelbase and presumably improved adhesion as the weight of the loco was spread evenly between them. The hydraulic clutch linkage was also a clear effort to avoid the earlier problems with a mechanical clutch. But it was to cause its own problems, primarily a frequent tendency to stall, including embarrassingly on one occasion when taking a train for President Chiang Kai-Shek up the mountain. This, and a lack of power meant the locos saw little use and on a 1966 visit to the line Charles Small observed that all four diesels *'spend all of their time in the shops.'* This second setback, combined with severe flood damage to the line in 1959, prompted a pause for reflection, for the next order for diesel power was not until 1962 and this time aimed firmly at the growing passenger traffic.

In 1962 two 250hp, 18 ton 25 seat diesel railcars with Cummins engines were supplied by Nippon Sharyo and proved an immediate success. Initially operating

DL2, one of two diesels built by Mitsubishi for mainline services in 1953, on display today in Beimen yard. They were not a success. 19 November 2016.

together, they shaved an hour off the then four hours required for the uphill journey. A further five, slightly more powerful, were brought into service in 1966 and three more in 1970. Trials showed that they were also capable of hauling two trailer cars and in this form were to provide the bulk of passenger services for the next decade.

Passenger traffic continued to grow, however, in line with the growing affluence of Taiwanese, while the Shays had now been in service for over half a century. Clearly something else was needed. In 1969 the railway returned to Mitsubishi who supplied five locomotives to the same basic external design as those of 1954 and 1955, including coupled wheels. This time however a more powerful 523hp engine and a much-improved transmission through a hydraulic drive torque converter and a series of cardan shafts appear to have overcome previous drawbacks. In this regard, the drive system bears an interesting similarity to the arrangement on the Shays, testimony indeed to the robustness of that design. The locomotives were an immediate success and went on to form the basic model for all subsequent orders, bar three. They were followed by a further four in 1972, finally enabling the Shays to be withdrawn from mainline duties. Capable of propelling four laden carriages up the mountain from Chiayi, they also gradually supplanted the railcars on passenger services and at least one railcar set was transferred to the Lotung line serving Taipingshan. All remained in regular service for the next thirty years or more. They were, however, the last locomotives to be ordered from Mitsubishi.

International politics decided the next order. By now Mitsubishi had a good understanding of the unique requirements for Alishan and the Forestry Bureau would almost certainly have been happy to place further orders with them. But as noted in the previous chapter, after Japan established diplomatic relations with China in 1973, the government in Taipei had imposed a boycott of Japanese products, so for the next order the Forestry Bureau turned to Orenstein & Koppel, who supplied three 650hp B'B' diesel hydraulics between 1975 and 1977. They were an unusual design, the bogies sitting inside the frames, suggesting perhaps a modification of a design intended for metre or even standard gauge use. No fewer than eight sandpipes were fitted, one for every wheel, suggesting that O&K were well aware of the challenges of the line.

The cabs were considerably more comfortable than those of the earlier locos, making them popular with crews, while the higher horsepower rating should have also made them attractive. Technically too, they were more advanced than the Mitsubishi locomotives but this was a very mixed blessing for it made them prone to breakdown. Sentiment about them was not improved after one was involved in a serious derailment in 1978 but the final nail in their collective coffin appears to have been an insistence by O & K that they alone must supply all spare parts, for which they quoted unacceptably high prices. Two locos were therefore cannibalised to keep the third in service but all three were withdrawn after only a few years. Thereafter, once the government had lifted its embargo, the Forestry Bureau turned back to Japan and the tried and tested Mitsubishi design, ordering a further six locomotives of this design, of either 25 or 28 tons' weight and 510 or 550 hp, from Nippon Sharyo between 1980 and 1982.

After a twenty-year gap in deliveries of new locos, the growth in tourist traffic led to a further three diesel locomotives being delivered from Nippon Sharyo in 2006 and another five, built locally by the Taiwan Rolling Stock Corporation, in 2007. This latter company is in fact a Nippon Sharyo subsidiary, established in October 2002, presumably to enable the company to win orders from the Taiwanese government. While externally similar to earlier stock, the 21st century locos are more powerful still, dispense with the external connecting rods in favour of internal gears and can push a 75-tonne loaded five car train uphill. According to the railway's management heavier trains would be possible and trains are limited to five cars not by weight but because of the curvature on the line and the locos pushing ascending trains uphill.

The tourist and emotional pull of the Shays has long been recognised by the Forestry Bureau. Of the 20 originally delivered, no fewer than 17 remained in use in 1970, the remaining three having been scrapped following accidents. In 1972 no 14 went to Australia's Puffing Billy Railway. Progressive withdrawal of the remainder, usually as their boiler certificates expired, saw most of them plinthed at various locations around Taiwan. At least one, no 26, (Lima works no 2789 of 1914) remained in working order at the formal end of steam working however and saw use thereafter on occasional steam specials. Although very infrequent, the success of these encouraged the Forestry Bureau to restore a further two, numbers 25 (Lima 2788) and 31 (Lima 2947) to working order. No 26 remains in 'as built' condition, coal-fired whereas the other two have been converted to oil-firing, with the further 'refinement' of electronic controls

One of three diesel locomotives supplied from Orenstein & Koppel in the mid-1970s, now on the scrap line in Chiayi yard, 19 November 2016.

and compressors, enabling steam to be raised quickly. No 26 now sees very little use, indeed in 2016 it was out of service at Chiayi both awaiting repair and also subject to a local authority ban on coal fires on environmental grounds. Numbers 25 and 31 have seen more frequent use. In 2007 regular scheduled weekend steam hauled trains were introduced between Chiayi and Jhuci. Although this was a welcome initiative, it was not well publicised, the trains were poorly patronised and the operation did not survive. Regular excursions behind Shays continue out of Alishan, however, mainly during the peak tourism season which coincides with the cherry blossoms in April. These are normally confined to short runs between Alishan and Zhaoping.

Rolling stock

Given that the primary traffic was always timber, the bulk of the goods rolling stock was low-sided bogie flats designed to carry logs. A standard 28 feet long design was introduced in 1918 and survived largely unchanged thereafter. A number were fitted with a brakeman's cabin at one end, one of which would be positioned at the uphill end of the train for signalling purposes (the loco was always at the lower end of the train). These were supplemented by large numbers of bogie bolsters, semi-permanently coupled by means of lengthy bars between them. These offered much more flexibility in carrying felled trees of varying sizes: if positioned carefully, loaded logs could overhang on curves to a greater degree than if loaded on a wagon. Several covered bogie wagons also of 28 feet length made up most of the remainder of the goods wagon fleet for most of the timber-hauling years.

The first passenger carriages by contrast were reminiscent of early quarrymen's carriages on some of the Welsh slate railways. 16 feet long and 9 feet high they were four wheeled with a single end door on each side and seated 18 in third class or ten in second. Introduced in 1914, they were probably only ever intended for short distance working, for the first bogie carriages were introduced in 1914. 27 feet long, they seated 30 passengers on longitudinal benches and were followed in 1920 by a similar version but this time with end balconies and seating 28. This was to form the basic design and layout of carriages for the next forty years although subsequent carriages would be 36 feet long and have enclosed vestibules. A number of replicas were built around 2005 for use on heritage services such as the Shay specials at cherry blossom time.

The next big change came in 1960 with the introduction of all-steel carriages, 9.75 metres long (10.6 metres over couplings), fully enclosed and with larger windows and access via a single end door or a centre door on each side. Several remain in existence. In 1973 the first ten new 'special passenger cars' were introduced. Externally similar to the 1960s' design, these featured adjustable seats to face the direction of travel for the first time, in place of the old fixed longitudinal benches.

The railway countered the advent of road competition in the early 1980s through the introduction of new passenger carriages for main line services offering a significantly higher level of comfort than previous carriages. Designated 'Special Passenger Cars' or SPCs, these must rank among the most luxurious on the 762mm gauge anywhere, with panoramic windows, air conditioning, reclining seats and toilets. All services over the main line are now formed solely of this stock, of which there are currently 36 carriages in service. The standard version weighs 11 tons, measures 11.3 metres over couplings and seats 25. The standard formation of a train is five such cars and to comply with Taiwanese legislation every train even has a dedicated breast-feeding room for mothers with infants in one of the carriages.

The nature of the 'sunrise trains' to Zhushan is very different, the journey being of no more than 10 – 15 minutes' duration. A dedicated fleet of 24 carriages was constructed for these services in the 1990s. Slightly shorter than the SPCs at 10 metres' body length, they are designed for maximum capacity, with longitudinal seating on either side and double entrance doors at each end of the carriage.

4

AMIDST THE EAGLES AND IMMORTALS: TAIPINGSHAN AND PAHSIENSHAN

The Alishan line is without doubt the best known of all Taiwan's narrow gauge lines but at the peak of the timber industry it was only one of six logging rail systems in the country, all but one of which remained in operation until at least the end of the 1970s. What they lacked in scale when compared to the sugar network, in total extent being barely one-third the length of the latter, they more than made up for in scenic grandeur and engineering and operating challenges. Today only the Alishan line survives in anything like its original extent and four of the systems have disappeared leaving little or no trace. Yet all were spectacular, with extensive use made of long aerial ropeways, cable-worked inclines and high, flimsy-looking trestles to access the stands of timber in the high mountains.

Timber Sledge, Mt. Hassen.　八仙山木馬ノ運村

Before the railways were built felled logs were brought down from the mountainside on toboggan paths or *mumadao*. This particular one was at Pahsienshan

taipics.com

Of the three major forest reserves initially identified by the Japanese, Pahsienshan, like Alishan, is on the west side of the island and of a similar height, rising to 2448 metres. At 1950 metres, Taipingshan in the north east is somewhat lower. Access to both is even more challenging than at Alishan. In each case, the initial approach to the mountain range is along a broad and fairly level river valley running inland, only for the way to then be blocked by a seemingly impassable mountain wall straight from an oriental brush painting, sheer peaks rising into the clouds and separated from one another by deep ravines. For railway engineers, they presented an even more formidable obstacle than Alishan.

In neither area were the stands of timber as dense as at Alishan but the quality was often higher. Again, cypress, Taiwanese hemlock and conifers, mainly spruce, were the main varieties. The cypress from Taipingshan was of particularly old growth and high quality and quickly became highly valued for the *doraemon* or main gates of Shinto shrines in Japan. Timber felling in each area started around 1915, about the same time as at Alishan. To begin with, in both areas the felled trees were dragged on wooden sledges along paths cut in the forests, the paths usually being improved by laying smaller logs transversely to make a rough guideway known as a *mumadao* (木馬道), literally, 'wooden horse way,' the wooden horses being the sledges. They were dragged in this way to a suitable spot on the mountainside where they were then dropped down long chutes improvised from the slope, again sometimes enhanced with logs, known as *xiuluo*(修羅) to a spot where they could be collected then floated down rivers to sawmills. As a procedure, it worked but apart from the dangers involved a high percentage of the timber was damaged as it tumbled down the mountainside or was lost in flash floods, something to which Taiwan's rivers are especially prone. In each case, the answer over time was to build a network of tramways, aerial ropeways and cable-worked inclines in the mountains to replace the slides, with a narrow gauge railway along the river valley to bring out the logs. Beyond this, the differences in operation on the two systems outweighed the similarities and the systems are best considered separately.

Taipingshan

The area known today as Taipingshan is a popular tourist destination, reached by a steep mountain road along which spectacular vistas of Taiwan's central mountain range open up as it twists upwards through a series of hairpin bends. It seems hard to believe that a railway ever penetrated these slopes. This is not the original Taipingshan, which lay on the other side of the mountain at a slightly lower altitude. The entire area was once the land of the Atayal aboriginal tribe and was not explored by the Japanese until 1914. But its potential as a source of high quality, old growth timber was immediately apparent and felling started the following year, when just under 9,000 cubic metres of timber was cut down. Access to the area was along the Lanyang River which flowed from a south westerly direction towards the coast, then up a tributary stream from a settlement at Tuchang. To begin with a camp was established close to the river on the western slopes of what came to be known as Taipingshan. Tuchang is about 400 metres above sea level and the original Taipingshan camp was some 1000 metres higher. When the water in the river was high enough, logs could

The overgrown remains of a *mumadao* at Taipingshan, 25 September 2016.

A 1972 view of the loco shed at Lotung showing 3 locos on shed, the stock of the mixed train and, in the background, the timber mill which was the mainstay of the line's traffic. The mixed gauge track in the foreground is the end of the 1067mm gauge siding from Lotung station. Note the extended bunker on No. 5 but not No. 2. The shed burned down in a fire in January 1979, a few months before the line closed.

Kurashige Nobutaka

be floated downstream to Tuchang where they were collected before being floated down the wider Lanyang River to the sawmill. Two mountain trails also gave access to the camp. Logging grew rapidly and by 1920 the output had more than doubled to 19,345 cu. metres.

Development of a hydro-electric project on the river in 1923 prevented its further use for floating logs downstream. Part of a railway line built for the construction of this was taken over on its completion and extended in each direction to make a 762mm gauge line from the small town of Lotung (now Luodong, 羅東) on the east coast, south west along the Lanyang River valley towards Tuchang, 35.8km away at the foot of the mountain wall. Work started in 1924 and the line opened in stages, reaching Tuchang two years later. Although built along a broad river valley and relatively level, so lacking the engineering masterpieces of the Alishan line, it was still a far from straightforward project. The valley sides were steep and prone to landslides while the river itself was subject to rapid rises in water level during and after typhoons. No fewer than 138 trestle viaducts were required, the longest over 400 metres, together with 7 tunnels. Elsewhere long stretches of the line were placed on embankments above the river bed. Although the 1067mm gauge North Coast railway had reached Lotung in 1919, the forestry line stopped 600 metres to the north at Jhulin, where a sawmill which was the destination for almost all the line's traffic was located and from where

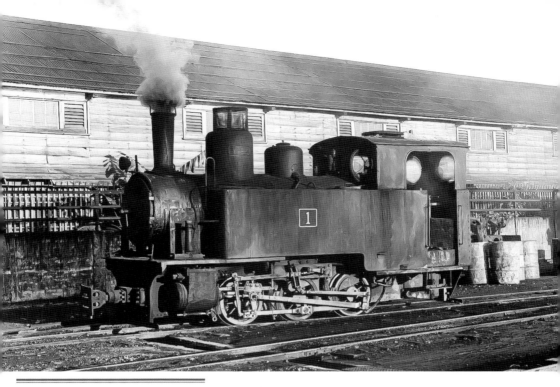

A classic view of No. 1 at Lotung. Note the builder's plate on the front dome, the spark arrester temporarily placed on the dome and the lack of extended bunker.

Kurashige Nobutaka

a 1067mm gauge siding provided a connection to the main line. The loco sheds and other facilities were built here. With no means of access to the Taipingshan area other than by rough footpaths the line also carried passengers, operating as a common carrier service from the outset on a public timetable. The new accessibility offered made Taipingshan immediately popular with tourists, a local newspaper proclaiming it one of the '8 most beautiful places in Taiwan' in 1927. Non-forestry traffic was clearly of secondary importance however, as passengers continuing beyond the sawmill had to make their own way between the stations at Jhulin and Lotung.

Three 15 ton 0-6-0Ts were delivered from Nippon Sharyo in 1923 in time for completion of the line to Tuchang and the start of public services over what became the Lotung Forestry Railway. Given that the primary aim of the railway was always to bring logs from Tuchang, where they were gathered after being brought down the mountainside, to the sawmill at Jhulin, the bulk of rolling stock was composed of three varieties of flat wagon: 22-foot-long full bogie wagons weighing 6 tons, 15½ foot long, 5 ton four wheel wagons and 9½ foot long 3 ton four wheel bolsters, used together for carrying the very largest felled trees. A number of 32½ foot long bogie passenger cars were also supplied. Weighing 10 tons tare, 12.5 tons fully laden, these could carry 40 passengers sitting on longitudinal bench seats with access from end balconies. At the time of opening, opportunities for agriculture in the river valley were limited so the villages were few and small and most passengers would be travelling in connection with the forestry industry. Intermediate traffic was accordingly sparse

By January 1979 just one loco, No. 2, remained in use. It is seen here being prepared for service before taking out one of the three daily mixed trains which survived to the very end. Built by Nippon Sharyo, the builder's plate can be seen on the steam dome.

Nicholas Pertwee

but seven intermediate stations were still provided for such traffic, with three trains daily to begin with, taking around two and one half hours to cover the 36km. From the beginning, most timber was carried on dedicated trains with mixed trains handling the remaining traffic, a pattern that was to remain with only minor changes until the very end of the line's operations.

Timber output from Taipingshan was already increasing steadily and with this rise in output tree felling moved steadily further away from the camp at Taipingshan and the limitations of the *mumadao* for removing the timber became ever more apparent. But initial improvements were incremental, rather than dramatic. The first step was to lay a guide rail down the middle of the wooden path. This allowed operators to stand in a safer position behind the logs, rather than in front where they risked being crushed should they slip or lose control. Upgrading the pathways or guideways to push-cart lines was the next logical step. In moves reminiscent of the development of the Ffestiniog railway in Wales these were initially operated by gravity, with water buffalo employed to haul rakes of the empty log bolsters back up the line. Completion of the railway line from Lotung to Tuchang was accompanied by an immediate jump in output, from 22,800 cubic metres (m^3) felled in 1926 when the line opened, to over 35,000 m^3 the following year. Except for some wartime years, annual output would not drop below 30,000 m^3 again until 1970 by when logging was starting to decline.

A 1977 view of no 2 on a mixed train.

John Tillman

The increase in output was met by an expansion and enhancement of the transport network. First, an aerial ropeway was constructed at Tuchang in 1924 to provide direct access to the push-cart lines and remove the need for logs to be dropped by chute. The first such system in Taiwan, it was the precursor of those at Alishan and would be followed by several more as logging expanded throughout the island. Secondly the rail network was extended ever further as the premium old-growth timber was sought out. Two long lines were built deep into the mountains from the Taipingshan camp, one in an easterly direction following the Jiancing stream, the other to the south, with accompanying branches. Each also required at least one additional ropeway, with more added as the system expanded. Clearly the old combination of gravity and water buffalo power for the expanding rail network was no longer adequate.

The initial response was the introduction of light internal combustion locos. This was possibly inspired by their success at Alishan but the Pahsienshan system was also receiving some around the same time so it is possible that all three deliveries were part of a centrally managed experiment or policy decision by the Forestry Bureau. At Taipingshan two 3 ton Plymouth petrol tractors built by Fate-Root-Heath were introduced in 1928, followed by another two in 1930. These were numbered P1, P2, P3 and P5. (The absence of a number 4 was deliberate and in accordance with oriental custom of avoiding its use where possible given the similarity of its pronunciation to that of the word for death. There is no record of a fifth loco and the subsequent, larger fleet of Kato tractors also lacked a number 4). They appear to have been a success as a further, larger tractor of 4.5 tons, this time from Kato of Japan, was supplied in 1932.

An unidentified loco on a Lotung – Tuchang train. All the locomotives faced towards Lotung.

Kurashige Nobutaka

Around this time, with the western slopes increasingly logged out, the decision was taken to move the centre of logging activities to an entirely new location on the eastern slope of the mountain, which would not only facilitate logging in that area but also open entirely new areas to the south and further east. The new camp would be some 7km from the old one as the eagles fly but considerably more when following the contours. By the 1950s Taipingshan would grow to become the largest forestry reserve by output of felled timber in the country and at the easternmost point timber felling was taking place 50km or so away from the original camp. Not only would it have been a challenge to bring all the felled timber out over such an extended system, the geography of the area is such that several more ropeways would almost certainly have been required to do so.

A new, direct access route from Tuchang to the new camp was therefore surveyed and built. The steepness of the mountains meant there was no question of a single rail link. Instead, a combination of three long aerial ropeways powered by large stationary steam engines and connecting rail lines was built giving direct access up the mountainside. While similar in concept to the ropeways already on the other side of the mountain and at Alishan, these were on a far grander scale. To minimise transhipment costs and delays the ropeways were designed to carry not only loaded timber wagons but also workmen's cars and even locomotives, all of which could be loaded direct onto the carrying mechanism. The ropeways were possibly unrivalled anywhere in the world at the time for their sheer length, the longest one being more than 1km, unsupported by intermediate pylons and with a vertical ascent of more than

Another 1972 view of no 2 heading a mixed train towards Lotung over one of the many trestles on the line.

Kurashige Nobutaka

460 metres. To ride on one must have been a spectacular, even frightening experience although not a single accident was recorded throughout the years of operation.

A 4.5km stretch of line was built from Tuchang, the terminus for public services on the valley line, to the foot of the first ropeway at Renze (or Rentse). This was built to logging railway standards, using 9kg/m rail rather than the 15kg/m of the 'main' line, over a 3% gradient, the steepest on the whole system. By Taiwanese norms this was not especially severe or unusual and it applied to unladen ascending trains. To gain height however, the line started with a switchback reversal out of Tuchang station, followed by a sharp reverse curve, all on the 3% grade. The first ropeway rose 356 metres on a single unsupported span of 950 metres before a further 3.92km of light railway connected to the second, highest and longest ropeway. One further ropeway was needed to reach Taipingshan, giving a total vertical ascent of 1250 metres. The ropeways and connecting lines together offered a single route from Tuchang to Taipingshan 16.25km in length. In comparison, the road that now climbs the mountain to Taipingshan in a series of hairpins is over 25km long.

The new Taipingshan camp quickly became the focal point of activity on the mountain. The Forestry Bureau established an administrative centre, dormitory accommodation was provided for the lumberjacks and in time it became a sizeable self-contained community, complete with school. Maintenance of the rail tractors was carried out here. Railways branched out in three directions: in addition to the main line from the north giving access to Tuchang via the ropeways, a line was built to the south and west and a new branch was gradually extended some 15km eastwards. The

Loco no 1 of the Lotung line, a Nippon Sharyo 0-6-0T of 1924, has been preserved on static display with a short demonstration train near the site of the old Tuchang station. Also preserved there and visible behind is a two car railcar set, originally built for the Alishan line but transferred to Lotung in 1970. 31 May 2008.

new ropeway system opened in 1935 and in anticipation of the increased traffic, two, possibly three, more 5 ton locos, also from Kato, were delivered in 1935 and 1936.[*] Production at the original site ceased in 1936, with all activity formally transferred to the new one from the following year.

Whether the railway lines based on the original camp ceased at the same time is less clear. Presumably those from the first Taipingshan camp towards Tuchang did so. But the most easterly of the early branches, known as the Jiancing line, came close to the line into the new camp. While there does not appear to ever have been a physical connection, transfer of logs by *mumadao* would have been quite possible. The uppermost section of this line can still be followed today on a short forest trail and even allowing for some cosmetic restoration of the track, it seems unlikely that track and timber bridges would be in anything like the condition they are today if the line had actually been closed for nearly eighty years. All the original locomotives were

---

[*]   The Taipingshan records show locos G2 and G5 (G for 'Kato') delivered in 1934 and 1935 respectively but G3, a smaller 4 ton loco, as delivered in 1942. The numbering sequence suggests this may have been a replacement for an earlier loco.

Sister loco no 15, most probably a Nippon Sharyo product, on display in Luodong Forestry Park at the head of a couple of replica carriages, 10 June 2016.

transferred to the new system. Forestry Bureau records show them all still in service in 1954, the oldest ones operating on the short stretches between the ropeways on the section from Renze to Taipingshan.

The limitations caused by both the ropeways and the steepness of the mountain sides in turn restricted the size and structures of the logging lines. The ropeways had a weight capacity of 5 tons, making this the maximum size of rail tractor that could be operated and the petrol tractors were limited to a maximum train of seven loaded wagons. With the amount of timber being felled in peak years it also meant considerable method and discipline was required to ensure the ropeways operated efficiently and backlogs of timber awaiting transport did not build up. With the forestry community at Taipingshan also relying on them, a timetabled passenger service was operated using dedicated passenger gondolas. These weighed 600kg. unladen or 1200kg. gross with 10 passengers on board. Photographs of their use suggest space inside was at a premium, with luggage and equipment being strapped to the outside. The first such gondolas had water tanks underneath which would be filled at the upper station of each ropeway to ensure sufficient counter-balancing weight of empty stock.

With timber traffic growing steadily and more presumably expected once the new logging station was open, the original locomotives on the Lotung Forestry Railway must have struggled to cope, even more so as one was written off in an early accident. In 1933 two additional locomotives were acquired followed by two more in 1941, all 0-6-0Ts of between 13 and 15 tons' weight.

As already noted, Taiwan suffered badly from the wartime dislocation of the economy and the subsequent occupation by China. Overall industrial and agricultural production in 1946 was less than half what it had been in 1937 and this was apparent in timber output at Taipingshan. From a peak output of 82,142 m^3 in 1943 it fell to just 12,500 m^3 in 1946 and the railway carried just 15,000 tons of freight in total that year. But like sugar, timber was of strategic importance, both for rebuilding in Taiwan itself and to earn foreign currency through exports. The system was expanded accordingly. A new line was built far to the east to exploit new areas of timber, with more ropeways and a cable-worked incline added accordingly in 1951 and 1952. 7 new petrol tractors were delivered in the same period, all from Kato and of 4.5 or 5 tons in weight. Timber production gradually recovered, eventually reaching an all-time high of 93,000 m^3 in 1959. The system was dynamic in the sense that lines in some areas were only extended when logging in other areas was exhausted.

Inevitably the increased output placed more demands on the Lotung railway, its motive power and rolling stock. Overall freight traffic peaked in 1955 at nearly 243,000 tons. The increased demand for timber meant increased employment in the mountains and the settlement at Taipingshan grew accordingly. Following the end of the Chinese civil war in 1949, some two million mainland refugees had fled to Taiwan and accommodating them was a priority. Many were re-settled in hitherto less developed areas along the east coast and in the eastern mountains, from which the previously sparsely populated valley of the Lanyang River was not exempt. While passenger traffic never again reached the 235,000 carried in 1949, throughout the 1950s over 150,000 were being carried annually and by 1959 the original three return mixed trains daily had grown to 7 up and 6 down trains daily, supplemented by morning and evening short trip workings between Tuchang and Wumen. Clearly, still more motive power was needed to cope with both this and the increased timber traffic.

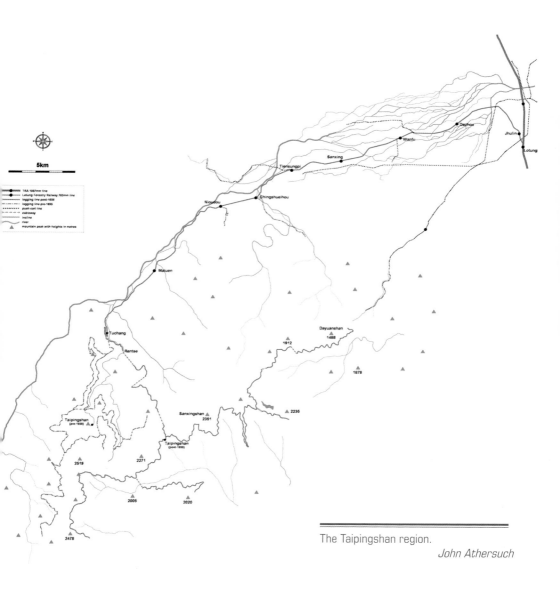

The Taipingshan region.

John Athersuch

Taiwanese sources record five additional locomotives, again all 0-6-0Ts supplied in 1958. These are generally recorded as built new locally by the Taiwan Machinery Company, which supplied a number of similar locomotives to the sugar corporation around the same time. Three of them ostensibly survive today on display at Jhulin although there is some doubt about both their actual provenance and when they were delivered, as explained in the section on motive power below.

1959 was the high point after which a gradual decline set in. Timber felling on the scale of that year was unsustainable. From the outset of logging in Taiwan the Japanese, and the Taiwanese after them, had followed a strict policy of rotational felling and re-planting, so timber supplies remained plentiful. But inevitably the premium value old growth timber had been largely logged out, while wider industrial

Access into the mountains was by a series of aerial ropeways, designed to carry loaded timber bolsters without the need for transhipment.

Taiwan Forestry Bureau

changes, especially in construction, were affecting demand. The equipment was ageing and road competition was rearing its head. Output declined steadily, if irregularly, throughout the 1960s. At the end of that decade timber felled was little more than half what it had been ten years earlier. By the early 1970s the line was facing numerous challenges.

At first the railway fought back. A direct link to Lotung main line railway station was finally built in 1970, improving convenience for passengers while a diesel railcar and trailers were brought from the Alishan line to provide a faster and more comfortable service, a new shed being built for them at Jhulin. (Previously some passenger carriages as well as steam locomotives had also made their way from Alishan to Lotung and in this respect the latter line appears to have been something of a poor relation, dependent on the elder sibling's hand-me-downs).

Although access to the forests remained restricted, there are several hot springs in the region, notably at Renze at the foot of the first ropeway and the railcar service was a brave attempt to provide a service for the growing number of tourists to these. But it was too little and too late. Construction of a road up to Taipingshan enabled the declining number of logs to be brought out by truck, avoiding the slow, cumbersome and ageing ropeway system which was finally closed in the mid-1970s. For a while the valley line soldiered on but after a typhoon caused considerable

The ropeways also conveyed specially designed workmen's carriages, capable of moving along the railways although in practice separate carriages were normally provided. Despite a somewhat cavalier approach to safety and loading, no major accidents were ever recorded on any of the Taiwanese ropeways.

Taiwan Forestry Bureau

damage to the civil works in the summer of 1979, it too succumbed, closing on 1 August 1979. Steam hauled mixed trains continued to provide a service to the very end, supplemented in the final years by the railcars. Non-timber traffic was always modest and in the last years trains were frequently no more than a single carriage and one or two wagons.

Motive power

The history of motive power for the logging lines is straightforward. 15 tractors of from 3 to 5 tons' weight were supplied from Fate-Root-Heath and Kato between 1928 and 1953. The first four were all 3 ton Plymouths, two delivered in 1928 and the other two in 1930. Thereafter 11 tractors were supplied by Kato, one in 1932, one in 1935, one in 1937, one in 1942 and the remainder in 1951 and 1952. The first and last of the Katos as well as two supplied in 1951 were of 4.5 tons' weight, the remainder were 5 tons. All the locos, whether Kato or Plymouth, appear to have been petrol-powered from the outset and appear to have remained so to the end of operations. (Early photos show what might be a tank for charcoal gas beside the footplate on some locos but others show locos filling up at what is very clearly a petrol pump). All but one also appear to have remained in service to the very end of logging at Taipingshan.

By contrast, the motive power for the Lotung Forestry Railway is shrouded in a fog of confusion, compared to which the debate over numbers of the Alishan Shays is a mere trifle. The detailed and comprehensive nature of so many of the relevant records makes it all the more puzzling. What is clear is that at the time of the line's closure in 1979 the highest numbered locomotive on the roster was 15, and eight locos which reputedly saw service on the line are today on static display at different sites around Taiwan. But there are at least four different accounts of their origins.

At the start matters are straightforward. Nippon Sharyo, which had begun locomotive manufacture in 1918, supplied three 15-ton 0-6-0 tank locos for the opening of the line. They bore works numbers 99-101 and the Nippon Sharyo works list shows them as being built in 1924. But this puts them out of sequence with both previous and subsequent locos so may be a misprint, 1923 being the more likely year of construction. They were given line running numbers 1 to 3 but following an accident in the early years, either number 1 (Nippon Sharyo 99) was written off and number 3 re-numbered, or parts of both locos were combined as a new no 1.

Okita suggests that Nippon Sharyo works number 104 of 1924 was also delivered to the line as number 4. This seems unlikely. Firstly, the Nippon Sharyo works list shows the customer as the Tongyang Electric Machine Company and second, as noted in respect of the loco-tractors, common practice in Taiwan was to avoid use of the numbers 4 and 10 because of their similarity in pronunciation to the word for death. There is no record of locos bearing either number on the line. But we shall come back to this.

With just two, or possibly three, locomotives available by the early 1930s the line must have been struggling to cope with growing traffic. In response, and presumably also in anticipation of the opening of the new ropeway system and new camp in 1937, two additional 0-6-0Ts were supplied in 1933. Both came second hand from the Alishan line, also under the control of the Forestry Bureau. These were two of the

Despite being closed for over 30 years, considerable evidence of the original logging lines at Taipingshan can still be seen, as in this view of rails and trestle bridges on the final approach to Taipingshan itself, 25 September 2016.

earliest locos for the line, whose size and design made them unsuited for the long, steep climb up to Alishan, no 1 (Andrew Barclay 1251) which reportedly became number 5 on being transferred to Lotung and the 21 ton Kawasaki 0-6-0T which became no 6 at Lotung. Okita describes no 6 as a 13 ton Kawasaki, built in 1914 and delivered new to Taiwan but without giving a works number for it. While a 13-ton loco would probably have been a more suitable fit for the Lotung line, in the absence of other corroborating information we can reasonably assume that no 6 did indeed come from the Alishan line, as is generally recorded in Taiwan.

Okita also lists no 7 as another 13 ton Kawasaki 0-6-0, supplied in 1935 but again without giving a works number and again I have found no supporting information for this in Taiwan, nor indeed any information as to the provenance of a no 7. What can be stated with confidence is that there were indeed two further locomotives supplied from Kawasaki, again 0-6-0Ts of either 13 or 15 tons bearing works numbers 2544 and 2545 and delivered in 1941, which duly became nos. 8 and 9 on the railway's roster.

Taking into account the write-off of one locomotive and the absence of a no 4, by 1942 there were therefore in theory seven locomotives in service. But if we discount the Okita record as a misprint or recording error, there is no record of a no 7 being delivered. On the other hand, the loco on static display today as no 5 bears no resemblance to an Andrew Barclay loco (see box), while photographs showing no 5 in use in the latter years of the line are of what is almost certainly a Nippon Sharyo locomotive. Nos. 6 and 7 are the only locos unaccounted for today, Lin Qing Chi in his history of the development of Taipingshan saying only that they were disposed of 'long ago.' Logic would suggest that if any locos were to be disposed of, the most likely candidates would be the oldest ones or those having least in common with the rest of the fleet. The two supplied second hand from Alishan in the 1930s fit both criteria: they were a decade or more older than the other locos and either came from a completely different manufacturer or were considerably heavier, so neither was a ready fit with the other motive power.

If we also bear in mind the frequency of errors in the official records, a plausible hypothesis is that the line did indeed receive four Nippon Sharyos around the time of opening, but with the fourth being allocated number 5, not 4 as stated by Okita, and that the locos subsequently delivered from Alishan were in fact numbered 6 and 7 but mistakenly recorded as 5 and 6. This would account for the gaps in numbers and the confusion over no 5. But pending a definitive explanation this must remain conjecture.

As timber output recovered in the aftermath of the post-war chaos, a need arose for additional motive power. In the years following the Chinese takeover in 1945 a further five locos came to the line. As already noted there was no number 10 so these duly became nos. 11-15 on the roster. But their origins and circumstances of arrival are shrouded in even more confusion than that surrounding locos 5-7. Three of them, nos. 11, 12 and 15, ostensibly survive today on display at the Forestry Park in Lotung, along with nos. 8 and 9, the two Kawasakis from 1941. According to the accompanying information boards all three were supplied new in 1958 and built locally by the Taiwan Machinery Company. The volume of traffic was almost certainly sufficient to justify extra locomotives, for in the late 1950s timber output was still expanding – 1959 was the record year, with over 93,000 m^3. felled.

But Okita suggests that the additional locos were all supplied in 1948 and comprised two locos built new that year, one by the Taiwan Machinery Co and one by Nippon Sharyo, two Nippon Sharyo 0-6-0Ts built in 1938 and transferred from the Taichung Light Railway, by this time also under the control of the Forestry Bureau (the Taichung Light Railway is covered in the next section, on Pahsienshan) and one of the Alishan 18 ton Shays.

A third view is advanced by Wei Zhi Hong in his history of the Pahsienshan line. He says that the Taichung Light Railway had 5 steam locomotives in 1956, all 0-6-0Ts of around 12 tons so similar in size to those at Lotung, to where he suggests all were transferred ahead of the replacement of the TLR line by a 1067mm gauge line. The official records only add to the confusion: the Transport Ministry records list just two steam locomotives on the Lotung line in 1950 but ten in 1970, without giving any further details in either case, while the Forestry Bureau has compounded it with its mis-recording of information (see box).

Lin Qing Chi offers the most logical explanation but is frustratingly incomplete in doing so. He says that locos 13 and 14 were supplied on loan from the Pahsienshan and Alishan lines respectively, while adding that it is not clear that either was ever returned, or what subsequently became of them. If Su Chao Hsu is correct about the second Barclay coming to the line in 1951 as noted in Chapter 3 – and the Alishan line records are considerably more thorough – then this would suggest that four of the five post-war deliveries came either then or earlier. We know too that the Taichung Light Railway had at least one Nippon Sharyo loco, probably more, although it also had its own traffic demands to cope with.

Of the three locos on display at Lotung today, one, no 11, bears external similarities with other locos known to have been built by the Taiwan Machinery Co. for use on sugar lines while both nos. 12 and 15 bear strong resemblances to Nippon Sharyo

A QUESTION OF NUMBERS – 2

Confusion over the history of the Lotung line motive power goes beyond that mentioned here and is unfortunately only exacerbated by official sources. A loco no 5 is on display today at the Chihnan Forestry Park near Hualien, behind an information board stating that it was built in the UK in 1911 (so consistent with being Andrew Barclay 1251). But it is very clearly a Nippon Sharyo product, not from Andrew Barclay. Photographs of no 5 in use in the latter days of the line also show a Nippon Sharyo locomotive, not an Andrew Barclay one and, like the one at Chihnan, with a protruding coal bunker behind the cab unlike most of the other Nippon Sharyo locomotives at Lotung. Given the location, however, it is possible that it came from the east coast railway which also had a Nippon Sharyo 0-6-0T, no 195 of 1928. Like LFR no.5, this also had a protruding coal bunker (see next chapter). So, either the loco fleet was renumbered at some point or, as hypothesised the Barclay was in fact assigned another number and erroneously recorded as no 5.

Another five locos from the line are currently on display in the Forestry Park in Lotung, nos 8 and 9 (both from Kawasaki), 11, 12 and 15. The latter three are confidently stated to have been built by the Taiwan Machinery Company in 1958. While identifying features such as builders' plates have been removed, anything more than the most cursory glance shows significant differences between them: in valve gear, tank design, chimney, cab spectacle plates and more. This seems unlikely if they came from the same builder, at the same time, to fulfil the same task and as part of the same order. Two of them bear more than a passing resemblance to Nippon Sharyo locomotives.

locomotives. So, the most plausible version of origins is a combination of all accounts: a newly built loco from the Taiwan Machinery Co in or around 1948 as no 11, two Nippon Sharyos supplied between then and 1951, at least one of them second hand from the Taichung Light Railway where it was surplus to requirements, the second Andrew Barclay from Alishan in 1951 where it was also surplus and a further Nippon Sharyo some time thereafter. But even this is far from convincing for the Nippon Sharyo works list shows just one loco supplied to the Taichung Light Railway, in 1925 and none at all to Taiwan in either 1938 or 1948 (the years Okita gives for construction of the post-war additions to the Lotung roster). Perhaps they were acquired second hand from one of the sugar lines as the latter received new post-war deliveries from Belgium. We can only hope that a definitive history of both the Lotung Forestry Railway and the Taipingshan logging lines will eventually shed light on the mystery and resolve the confusion.

The system today

Following closure, the ropeways were quickly removed but the logging lines were left derelict *in situ*. With the ending of commercial logging soon after, a decision was taken to turn Taipingshan into a forest park. The old administrative facilities have been converted into a centre for the park and a 3.2km stretch of the south-western branch line was rebuilt to carry tourists, using locally made diesel locos reminiscent

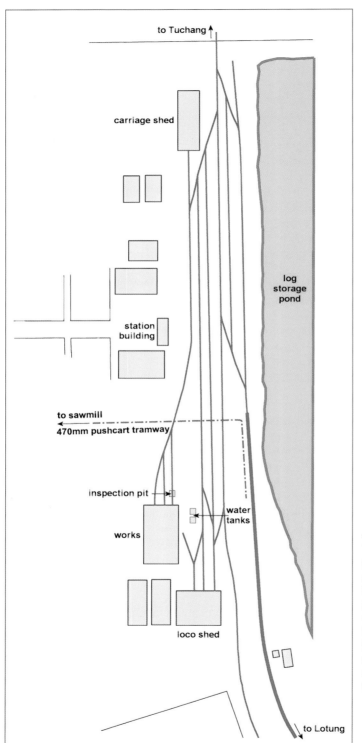

to Tuchang

carriage shed

log
storage
pond

station
building

to sawmill
470mm pushcart tramway

inspection pit

water
tanks

works

loco shed

to Lotung

The track layout at Jhulin station. A 1067mm gauge siding provided a direct interchange with the government railway while a 470mm gauge push-cart line for transferring timber and finished wood products to and from the adjacent sawmill meant the station boasted three different gauges.
From Lin Qing chi: 太平山開 發史 (Taipingshan Kaifanshi – History of Taipingshan Development)

Following the end of logging operations, a short stretch of one of the Taipingshan lines was rebuilt and re-opened as a tourist line using locally built diesel locos and modern toastrack carriages. Seen here in typical north Taiwan weather on 31 May 2008, the line has since closed due to landslide damage. It is not clear whether it will ever re-open.

of the original loco-tractors, hauling trains of semi-open toast-rack carriages. This line proved very popular and at peak periods long queues for the train would often form at Taipingshan. Unfortunately, landslide damage following typhoons has made considerable areas of the Taipingshan complex unsafe and has also undermined the permanent way in several places. The station is in the affected area and the line is therefore currently closed. It remains unclear whether it will ever re-open. Beyond the southern terminus of this line the old track remains in place, badly distorted as the result of earthquake damage, and can be followed for a further 2km or so to the site of one of the 1950s ropeways. Some 0.9km of the former Jiancing branch has also been restored and incorporated into a forest trail, just off the main road about 2km north of the Taipingshan complex. 40 years of tropical rainfall, typhoons and other natural events mean that most of the rest of the system has now disappeared into the vegetation but remains of old trestles with the rails still on them are clearly visible on the final approach to Taipingshan. Most of the eastern logging branch, the Sanxingshan line, has been converted into a scenic drive and footpath while the sites of at least two of the ropeway stations are also apparent. One now hosts a visitor centre for the mountain.

Some of the landslide damage to the tourist line at Taipingshan, seen from the site of Taipingshan station, also damaged and now closed off. 25 September 2016.

The site of the sawmill and Jhulin station at Lotung has been preserved in its 16-hectare entirety as the Luodong Forestry Conservation Park, the former log storage pond now a wetland wildlife area. Five of the original locos have been put on static display here: numbers 8, 9, 11, 12 and 15, which along with no 2 were the last locomotives remaining in use when the line closed. No 15 heads a short rake of rebuilt passenger carriages in front of the Jhulin station building and no 8 a demonstration train by the log-drop into the storage pond, with the other three under cover nearby. The whole park is very attractively laid out and a popular spot for locals at weekends and holidays. Loco no 2 is on a plinth in a park elsewhere in Lotung. North of Jhulin station the track bed is still very apparent for 150 metres or so before disappearing under new roads and other construction. Almost all the intermediate roadbed has disappeared through flooding or construction but three of the original station buildings survive, now converted to other uses. That at Dazhou forms part of the local community centre, with a short stretch of track in front to highlight its provenance but the most complete and nearest to original is at Tiensungpi, where a water tower and turntable have also been preserved as reminders of the railway.

At the other end of the line at Tuchang, the original brick and concrete station building survives. The road to Taipingshan now runs through the middle of what was

The restored Jhulin station building in Luodong Forestry Park, 10 June 2016.

once the station yard and on the other side, roughly where the logging line to Renze started, another loco, said to be no 1, together with a demonstration mixed train plus the railcar and trailer from Alishan are on display, while the challenges the original surveyors and builders faced remain very evident from the drama of the scenery. And as noted a further loco reputedly from the line is on display at the Chihnan Forest Park near Hualien.

Pahsienshan (八仙山)

The largest forestry reserve in Japanese days was at Pahsienshan, or 'Eight Immortals' Mountain' north east of the city of Taichung. Although the density of forest was not as great as at Alishan, the quality of the timber, red cypress especially, was higher. The area's proximity to a river also made access and removal of cut logs easier while lesser quality wood growing at lower levels was an important commercial source of firewood for charcoal production. Somewhat surprisingly given both the size of the area and quality of timber, exploitation of the reserve was not under the control of the Forestry Bureau but left initially to private enterprise. As at Taipingshan, at first felled trees were dragged along the mountain slopes to crude chutes, themselves formed from felled logs, from where they could be dropped to the Dajia river along which they were then floated downstream. Again, this procedure damaged the timber while repeated attacks on loggers by the local Atayal tribe also caused problems. As at Alishan, railway access would not only make exploitation of the timber resources easier but would also facilitate police and troop movements.

In contrast to both Alishan and Taipingshan which were in relatively remote areas, Pahsienshan lay not far from Taichung, today Taiwan's third city and a major town even in the early Japanese period. The immediate vicinity is relatively flat and while never reaching the scale of cultivation further south, the planting of sugar cane was expanding and with it the growth of neighbouring settlements. With this came a demand for improved transport facilities and in August 1913 the Taichung Light Railway Company (台中輕鐵株式會社, in Japanese *Taichu Keitetsu Kaisha*) was established to develop push-cart lines in the area. The region around Taichung was well suited to these and it was eventually to become one of the larger push-cart companies on the island, with a network by the mid-1920s of more than 100km, the longest line being over 26km. Although the government records show these as of 495mm gauge (1ft 7½in.) they were very likely built to 545mm gauge (1ft 9½in. – see box in Chapter 1). Although many of the push-cart companies were Taiwanese owned, both its size and other factors point to this being a Japanese owned company. Its operations were similar in many ways to those of tramway and interurban railway companies in Europe and the USA around the same time. A spot on the Dajia River was developed as a small park with bathing facilities, for example, presumably in an effort to encourage leisure traffic, and its lines also opened up access to several hot springs in the mountains.

The company differed from most push-cart operations in one important respect, however, which was that one of its lines, starting from Fengyuan (豐原), a station 14km north of Taichung on the 1067mm gauge government railway and running eastwards for 11.7km to Tuniu (土牛) on the Dajia river, was built to 762mm gauge. The main settlement along the valley was at Tungshih, across the river from Tuniu. Rather than crossing the river to here, however, the railway continued along the left bank 1.4km beyond Tuniu to a terminus at Zhumuchang (貯木場, literally 'wood storing place') where the locomotive running shed and maintenance facilities were located. The name no longer appears on maps and indeed was later changed to that of the immediate locality, Hesheng, suggesting that it was chosen because the felled timber being floated downstream was already being gathered here. Passengers for Tungshih had to make do with a push-cart connection from Tuniu. The line also connected at the Fengyuan end with another push-cart line belonging to the company; clearly other traffic was in mind in constructing the line to this gauge, namely timber traffic from Pahsienshan.

Timber extraction from the forests here had been growing steadily since 1915. Although initially dependent on toboggan paths or *mumadao,* the first push-cart line may have been constructed as early as 1917, after which the railway continued to expand, initially as a push-cart line along the path of the *mumadao*. There was a continuous *mumadao* route from Tuniu to the forests by 1925 and by late 1927 this had been converted throughout into a railway, connecting with the Taichung Light Railway at Zhumuchang and allowing timber traffic to be taken through to Fengyuan, where a second wood storage facility was established a little way south of the station on the government railway.

Pahsienshan – an early coloured postcard view of a logging train on one of the high mountain lines behind one of the 4 ton Plymouth locos.

National Central Library of Taiwan

Although a through route was thereby established, the operating and traffic conditions divided it in practice into three distinct sections under two separate ownerships. In contrast to the Lotung Forestry Railway, whose *raison d'etre* was always the transport of felled timber from Taipingshan, the wide valley of the Dajia river was well-populated and generated considerable traffic for the Taichung Light Railway. Ten intermediate stations were provided between Fengyuan and Tuniu and the 1939 timetable shows 14 round trips daily taking between 39 and 43 minutes. Buses run between the two places much more frequently today but scarcely any more quickly in view of traffic congestion in Fengyuan. Such is progress!

As far as Tuniu the river valley is broad and relatively level and engineering works on the Taichung Light Railway were minimal. The maximum gradient was a moderate 1.6%, the sharpest curve a relatively gentle 200 metres radius and 12kg/m. rail was used. At Zhumuchang/Hesheng operational control passed to the Pahsienshan Forest railway. As the name implies, from here onwards the railway was laid more to logging railway standards, with lighter 9kg/m. rail. But the nature of the route changed dramatically too. Although a connection between the two lines was established here, the river valley narrows considerably and the railway needed to gain height rapidly to stay above the flood level. A long zigzag connection was built to enable it to do so. Quite why it was so long is a puzzle, for the line reversed direction for over 1.5km in the course of which it gained very little height; presumably it was dictated by operational requirements including the unloading of timber.

The approach to Pahsienshan along the Dajia River valley today. The railway hugged the embankment on the right. The power station dominating the photo was built in the mid-1950s and a proximate cause of the closure of the line. 28 May 2016.

The Xinshan cable-worked incline near Jiuliangqi, showing clearly the significant curve. As a result of a forest fire it saw barely ten years' use.

Taiwan Forestry Archives

South and east of Tuniu the valley narrows and the mountains close in quickly, leaving the railway no option but to hug the river on its rather circuitous second leg, a further 45km beyond Zhumuchang along the valley to Jiuliangqi (久良栖), on what came to be known as the Dajia River line. Gone were the easy conditions west of Tuniu. This section of track had the steepest gradient on the entire route between Fengyuan and Pahsienshan at 4.1% and curves of just 20 metres radius. In due course Jiuliangqi was to become the headquarters of forestry operations. Here the cut logs were collected, measured and recorded before being shipped out by train to Fengyuan although there are suggestions that some logs continued to be floated downstream even after completion of the railway, possibly because of their size.

Once at Jiuliangqi the mountains rose almost sheer and further progress by a conventional railway was out of the question. The line continued just over 1.5km to a point where two long aerial ropeways broken by a short intervening section of rail, the first 1.15km and the second 1.28km, took the line high up the mountainside. From here a 16km long line followed the contours before yet another ropeway, this time of 500 metres, led to the highest logging line, 14km in length. These mountain lines were often even more lightly laid, using 6kg/m rail but while curves in the mountains were again a minimum 20 metres radius, the ruling gradient was a slightly less severe 3.0%. Chutes or skids were again used to bring logs to the railway and in at least one case, a further *mumadao*, 6km long. As if the ropeways alone were not sufficient, old photos also show trains on high and very spindly looking wooden trestle viaducts. Without doubt, in terms of spectacle it must have been at least the equal of the lines at Alishan and Taipingshan.

Although the forestry railway made a direct connection with the Taichung Light Railway the two were operated as very distinct entities. As already noted, the main shed and facilities for the latter were at Zhumuchang while those for the forestry line were at Jiuliangqi. Furthermore, the different circumstances of the forestry lines east and west of Jiuliangqi called for different operating patterns and requirements.

While timber was always the principal traffic south and east of Tuniu, a major sugar cane nursery irrigation project was developed along the river valley in the 1920s. This included the construction of a hydro-electric dam and accompanying irrigation canals at Baileng which opened in 1928. Given the amount of infrastructure involved and the difficulties of access to upper reaches of the valley the railway was almost certainly used in its construction. Overgrown rock cuttings can still be seen in the vicinity of the dam. The Forestry and Agriculture Departments also developed a major plant nursery near Tuniu, served by its own extensive push-cart system. But while the forest railway appears to have offered a public passenger service, in terms of frequency this was very different to that between Fengyuan and Tuniu.

As if to emphasise the difference, in the November 1939 timetable just two of the 14 daily trains on the TLR continued beyond Tuniu to Zhumuchang, even though the running shed was here. There was just one train in the morning and one in the afternoon and the brevity of the turn round at Zhumuchang – three minutes in the morning and a mere two in the afternoon – suggested they may have been operated by a railcar or that locos changed at Zhumuchang: entirely possible as this was where the main shed was. In each case the train then waited considerably longer at Tuniu before continuing to Fengyuan. At Zhumuchang they appear to have provided a connection to and from a single daily train from there to Jiuliangqi, provided by a petrol railcar and taking 3 hours 40 minutes to cover the 45km. The railcars appear to have been small, four wheel affairs, reinforcing the view that passenger traffic was limited. What passenger traffic there was appears to have been mainly as far as an aboriginal settlement about three kilometres before Jiuliangqi.

Timber traffic was another matter. It was never as great as at Taipingshan, the amount felled in a year typically varying between around one-half and two-thirds the volume cut there but completion of the railway had a dramatic impact on the ability to ship the felled timber. In 1915, the first year of logging, just 836 m^3 of timber was shipped out but with completion of the rail link this rose to more than 15,000 m^3 in 1927. By 1930 more than 19,000 m^3 was being transported annually, with a peak of 43,790 m^3 in the war year of 1943. As at Alishan and Taipingshan, as timber was felled, so the lines were extended or new ones added to exploit further timber stands. Perhaps the most spectacular of all such extensions was at Pahsienshan where in 1938 the decision was taken to cut timber from Xinshan, a steep peak to the south-east of Jiuliangqi. From a junction about 1km south of Jiuliangqi, a long cable-worked incline took off to the east in a vertical ascent of several hundred metres. Photos show both a significant curve on the incline and at least one wooden trestle viaduct to maintain the grade. Given its length and steepness, using it must have required at least as great an act of faith as using the Taipingshan ropeways! Further access to the timber stands from the top of the incline was by *mumadao.* But a large forest fire on Xinshan in 1948 appears to have put a premature end to felling there and with it the incline, which had a working life of just ten years.

The system remained under private management until 1942 when the forest railway was taken over by the Forestry Bureau, remaining under its management thereafter. The Taichung Light Railway was also taken under government control during the war, but by that of the national transport company, not the Forestry Bureau. This supposedly led to friction between the two, each with different transport objectives in mind and was no doubt exacerbated by wartime shortages. On 1 June 1947, the lines were brought under the unified control of the Forestry Bureau. To begin with at least, operations appear to have continued much as before. The February 1952 timetable still showed 14 trains in the down direction (to Tuniu) and 13 up, the fastest taking 38 minutes but two slower ones in each direction taking an hour. Now however, eight down trains continued to Zhumuchang, renamed Hesheng, with seven starting from there, with a further three short workings in each direction between Tuniu and Putse, a station 3.7km before Fengyuan where a junction was at one time made with a 762mm gauge sugar mill line that provided a very circuitous link into Taichung.

In 1956 construction work started on the first cross-island highway, which followed the same river valley before climbing steeply into the mountains. To help with the construction work, a new 1067mm gauge branch line of the TRA was built from Fengyuan to Tungshih, on the north side of the river across from Tuniu. This section of the 762mm gauge line was closed at the same time and a new transfer point between the two gauges established at Meitse, a little way downstream from Tuniu where the two lines converged. Construction of a hydro-electric dam and reservoir higher up the valley after opening of the highway reduced the forestry area. With the volume of cut logs now much reduced, their removal by road was also facilitated by the opening of the highway and rail services ceased by 1959. All logging ceased the following year and by 1963 all equipment and Forestry Bureau personnel had been withdrawn. It was the first of the major forest reserves to cease felling. The TRA

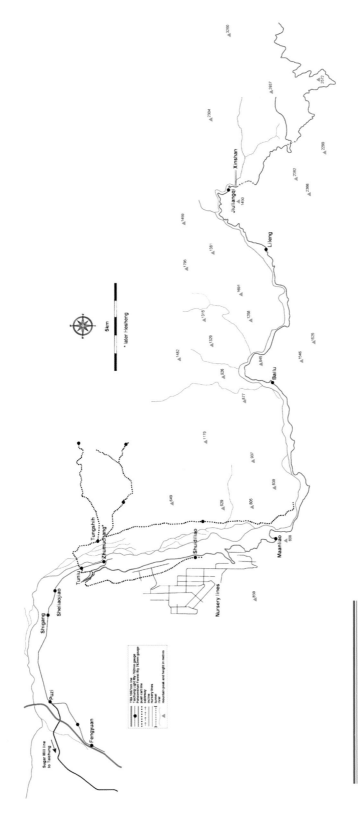

Pahsienshan and the Taichung Light Railway.

John Athersuch

branch itself closed to passengers in 1991 and completely in 1997 when the main line north from Fengyuan was relaid on a new alignment. Its track bed is now a cycle trail.

The 762mm gauge line has now been closed for more than fifty years, during which time Taiwan has undergone a major transformation and much of the route of the line has been obliterated by development. Some of the old station buildings at or near Jiuliangqi remain, however, in one case with the remains of a platform still evident outside, while sections of the track bed now form part of the network of hiking trails around Pahsienshan. The stationmaster's house at Tuniu still exists, albeit much modified, while the site of the station at Tuniu has been made into a small park, complete with a short section of track and information boards about the history of logging at Pahsienshan. But the most remarkable surviving element lies a short distance away, in the entrance to a housing compound not far from the main road. Here, half buried in the entrance way, is the unmistakeable remnant of a narrow gauge railway, a short section of track no more than 5 metres or so in extent. Even more intriguingly, it is not 762mm but 545mm gauge, suggesting it may have survived here since push-cart days, at least 70 years ago!

Motive Power

As in the case of Taipingshan, there is a striking disjuncture in the information available about the motive power of the Taichung Light Railway and that of the Pahsienshan logging lines. It is possible that services on the former were initially provided by push-cart in common with the company's other lines but the Nippon Sharyo works list records a 13 ton 0-6-0T, works no 141, being delivered to the line in 1925. The previous year Orenstein & Koppel had supplied a 13 ton 70hp 0-6-0T, works no. 10851, to Taiwan via their Japanese agent, which appears to have come to the line. It was described as a wood burner and as noted above, firewood was a significant local product; in 1928 this was recorded as being a bigger source of revenue than timber within Taichung province generally.

Thereafter, a fog of mystery and confusion descends. Okita states that three 70hp 0-6-0Ts were supplied by O&K but without providing builder's numbers and there are no obvious candidates in the O&K works list. And as noted previously, it seems highly probable that one or more Nippon Sharyo locos worked here before being transferred to Taipingshan. But as with O&K, there are no obvious candidates in the builder's records. Transport Ministry records suggest there were three locomotives on the line in 1950 and 1953 Forestry Bureau records also list 3 steam locomotives but without giving further details. But this seems too small a number given the volume of traffic. In 1950 over 580,000 passengers and nearly 55,000 tons of freight were carried, for example, which seems beyond the capability of just 3 locomotives. Nor is there a suggestion that there were ever railcars on the Hesheng-Fengyuan section. And Wei Zhi Hong says there were 5 steam locomotives on the line in 1956 which seems a more plausible number without, however, giving their origins.

We can only assume therefore that additional locomotives were obtained second-hand, maybe from the sugar lines although a possible source of O&K locos may have been the Ryobi Light railway in Japan, also 762mm gauge, which apparently took delivery of O&K 0-6-0Ts works numbers 10876 and 10877 in 1924 but was electrified just three years later. It is also possible that Otto Reimers and Co., O&K's agents in

Japan, supplied locos from a small stock they appear to have held for orders although in this case they are more likely to have been 0-4-0Ts, not 0-6-0Ts.

Meanwhile, photographs from 1926 show trains of hikers or visitors to Pahsienshan both being pushed by coolies in traditional push-cart fashion and also hauled in trains headed by small Plymouth industrial internal-combustion locomotives, suggesting that mechanical power had been introduced into the mountains even before completion of the link with the Taichung line. As at Taipingshan, internal combustion locos were the mainstay of operations in the mountain section east of Jiuliangqi throughout the lifetime of the railway, where the long aerial cableways meant that light locomotives were *de rigeur*. For reasons that may never become clear, two types of loco were ordered, of 4 tons and 7 tons in weight, readily distinguishable from one another by the full and relatively spacious cab on the latter compared to the rudimentary protection on the former. Weight restrictions excluded the latter from the ropeways and they were therefore confined to operations around Jiuliangqi. By 1956 there were 14 4 ton locos of 30hp. for work in the mountains and 11 of 7 tons and 46hp. for use around Jiuliangqi. Both types appear to have been supplied from Fate-Root-Heath's Plymouth works; an early photo of one of the 7 ton locos also shows a plate for Otto Reimers, the Tokyo agents for O&K, prominently displayed so presumably they also acted on behalf of Fate-Root-Heath.

But 7 tonners were presumably not considered suitable for the line between Tuniu and Jiuliangqi at this stage of diesel technology and experience. While this section was still formally part of the logging railway, the 45km length was considerably longer than the Plymouths were designed for and the combination of steep gradients, tight curves and relatively long distance called for something more powerful but still light enough for the 9 kg/m track. The records show that the specifications for both the Dajia River and Tuniu-Fengyuan lines required locos capable of hauling trains of 7 bogie wagons or 14 bolsters laden, or 18 bolsters unladen, at a speed of 9km/hour. In a bold move given the state of the technology at the time, internal combustion was chosen for this section too, the first time it was used in Taiwan over such length.

There appear to have been three locos built specifically for this work, of around 15 tons' weight and two-axles, photographs showing a central jackshaft linked by coupling rods to the two axles. After operation of the Taichung Light Railway was taken over by the Forestry Bureau in 1947, however, through running of log trains from Jiuliangqi to Fengyuan appears to have become the norm. The eleven 7 ton locomotives on the books in 1956 seems a generous number for shunting and short trip working around Jiuliangqi and with improvements to engine specifications in the interim, plus the possible addition of larger fuel tanks, it seems reasonable to assume that by this time the 7 ton locos were also being used on Dajia River line trains and maybe working through to Fengyuan. Kato supplied a large order of 18 loco tractors to the Forestry Bureau in October 1951. Three were small 4.5 ton models but the remainder were 7 ton versions so it is possible that these were added to the fleet at Pahsienshan and used on through running from the outset.

If this was the case, it would also help explain why some or all the steam locomotives from the Taichung line might have been transferred to Lotung as surplus to requirements, especially if railcars also took over passenger train services. Once more the official records tantalise in the information they reveal, giving only overall fleet numbers but not manufacturer or principal place of use. As in the case of locomotives on the Lotung Forest Railway, we must hope that further research will shed light on the mystery in due course.

5

SLEEPING CARS AND SWITCHBACKS – THE EAST COAST (HUATUNG) LINE

Taiwan's east coast towns of Hualien and Taitung are today popular holiday destinations. At peak periods trains leave Taipei for Hualien at ten minute intervals, the fastest taking just 2 hours for the journey of over 200km and continuing the further 170km to Taitung in another 1 hour 40 minutes, all on 1067mm gauge, some of it still single line. Those who wish can carry on and make a complete circuit of Taiwan by train within a day. For most passengers, however, the main concern about the journey is getting tickets as demand often far outstrips availability, especially at holidays and weekends.

It is all a far cry from the 1970s and before, when travel to and along the east coast was a far from straightforward proposition. Major geographical barriers hindered easy communication. The high mountains form a near impenetrable barrier to the west and reach almost to the shore, with cliffs blocking access to the north. Good natural harbours are non-existent. The east coast bears the brunt of Taiwan's frequent typhoons, further restricting access. Hualien, the principal city on the coast, was not connected with Taipei by railway until 1980 while to the south Taitung, the second city on the coast was only joined to the west in the final link of the railway's circumnavigation of the island in 1992. A series of tunnels, the longest over 8km in length, was needed as part of this.

In Chinese colonial times the region was the domain of often hostile aboriginal tribes and never under government control. The tribes were in the habit of murdering Japanese and other sailors who were shipwrecked along the coast and Chinese inability to do anything to prevent this was one reason for Japan taking the island from the Chinese in 1895. So the region has always seemed remote to Taiwanese.

But the mountains were a source of timber and the soil and climate offered considerable potential for agriculture. While the mountains and cliffs hinder access to the outside, a long valley a short way inland from the coast and running north-south, known locally as the East Rift Valley, makes a ready route for safe communications within the region.

As with development of the sugar industry and the opening up of the central mountains through construction of the Alishan line, serious consideration was first given to developing the region in the aftermath of Japan's war with Russia in 1905. In 1908 the Japanese Diet (Parliament) gave approval for the construction of a 762mm gauge line from a point on the coast at Hualien, south towards Yuli (Tamasoto to the Japanese), 90km away in the rift valley. Work appears to have started almost straight away but all material had to be brought in by sea and at this time the 'port' at Hualien was no more than a shallow bay in which larger ships could be unloaded by lighter. It is not clear whether it was a government built line from the outset or

Although most steam locomotives on the Huatung line were tank engines, bunker first running appears to have been exceptional, as this photo of an unidentified 0-8-0T on a turntable suggests. Until the 1960s the railcar fleet was single-ended, further necessitating the use of turntables. March 1966.

M Umemura

originally privately owned but construction was slow and as with the Alishan line, and indeed the principal west coast railway, if the line was not already under government ownership it was certainly taken over before it was finished, presumably as part of wider policy on control of the railways. It was eventually completed to Yuli in 1919.

Meanwhile to the south the Taitung Sugar Company had been established to develop a sugar mill north of the town. As with some of the other sugar mill railways it is not entirely clear whether the primary purpose was this or the operation of a public railway, for it started by constructing a railway line from a point near the shore in what is now Taitung, north along a river valley for some 42km. The 1922 records show it as operating just 10km of private line in addition to this, while its locomotive roster showed an equal number of locos (three) for both public and company operations. The line was reportedly completed by 1919 but was only opened to passenger traffic in April 1922. Later that same year it was taken over by the government railways with the intention of joining the two separate lines and work started on building a link to cover the 41km gap. The 174km through route between Taitung and Hualien was finally completed and opened to traffic in early 1926. Although government owned from the beginning – a works photo from the Vulcan Iron Works of one of the first locos has the wording 'Imperial Taiwan Railways' displayed prominently on the tank side – early management may have been on a quasi-autonomous basis for not until 1938 does the system appear to have been formally subsumed into the government railways.

Initial construction was very much on light railway principles, following river valleys as far as possible and keeping civil engineering to a minimum. The local geography

LDT103, one of the four 2-8-2s delivered from Nippon Sharyo in 1941, on a typical freight train, the first four wagons carrying sugar cane, March 1966.

M Umemura

in any case meant the requirement for major infrastructure was limited. By narrow gauge standards the gradients were fairly modest, the steepest being 2.5% in both directions over a summit a little way to the north of Taitung on the original sugar mill line. This was the same as the steepest gradient on the government 1067mm line and also the steepest gradient on any sugar line. There was just one tunnel, 1116 metres long, north of Yuli. This apart, the main civil engineering works were several long bridges across the wide river beds typical of the region, eight being 500 metres or more in length. Several of these were built as dual purpose road-rail bridges, also serving the coastal highway which ran parallel or close to the railway for much of its way. At the time of opening the line also had the longest distance between two stations on the entire Taiwan railway network, just over 8km between Fengtian and Hsikou. This may have been because the area was sparsely inhabited, or more likely was due to the presence in the vicinity of several push-cart lines which offered a more local service.

Despite the relatively modest gradients, there were no fewer than three switchbacks. From north to south these were at Hsikou, between Hualien and Fenglin on the northern side of one of two particularly wide river crossings, at Taoyeh (renamed Chiafeng from 1971 and now Luye) and Binlang. The latter two were either side of the summit, a little way north of Taitung. These were not conventional switchbacks or zig-zags however, but sidings used for crossing trains, the layout being dictated by the local geography. At Binlang and Hsikou, rather than using a conventional passing loop and requiring the train in the loop to re-start its train on the steep grade, uphill trains which had to cross others would run through the station then reverse into the

From a superficial glance, LDK52 would appear to be from the same makers as LDK 57. But it was from a different continent, being Porter works no 5645 of 1915. Seen here waiting for the right of way with a train of sugar cane, it was withdrawn in 1979. March 1966.

M Umemura

passing siding, which was above the through line and on or near the level, so much easier for re-starting the train. At Taoyeh uphill trains would run straight into the station then reverse out afterwards but into a siding on the level with the through line, again making the re-start easier. The layout at Hsikou was dictated by the need to gain height for the river crossing.

Even as a unified whole the railway was isolated. The road network remained very rudimentary (the standard of the road link between Hualien and the north continues to be a contentious issue in Taiwan to this day) and almost all freight, inbound and outbound, came by sea to and from Hualien or Taitung. The railway accordingly served more as a feeder to the two harbours than as a through route. Nevertheless, it soon served its purpose in opening up the region. In 1922, even before the two lines were joined up, over 560,000 passengers and nearly 150,000 tons of freight were carried on the northern line, an eleven-fold and sevenfold increase respectively on the figures for 1914, the first year of operation. 25 passenger cars and 150 goods wagons were available to meet demand. To judge by the recorded capacity, the majority of the former were designed to accommodate considerable amounts of passengers' luggage or general merchandise in addition to the passengers themselves: the only all first-class carriage had just 12 seats although in all likelihood it was a brake composite, as four first and second class composites each had thirty seats. Two third class carriages had 48 seats while 13 had just 18 seats. Presumably these too were either brake composites or also carried baggage, to account for their otherwise apparently roomy nature compared to other carriages.

Traffic on the Taitung sugar company's line to the south was rather more modest and more in line with conventional narrow gauge railways, 25,700 passengers and 1,835 tons of general freight being carried in 1922, the last year of separate operation, together with 17,600 tons of 'company freight.' This could have been sugar but may also have been material for construction of the railway. The line had just four passenger carriages and nine wagons for general freight.

Traffic grew steadily over the ensuing years. Completion of the northern line made access to the Lintianshan forest area easier. Although this did not enter full production until 1939, once it did almost all the output was shipped away by rail, mainly to serve a paper mill further up the coast. In due course sugar mills were opened at Malan, north of Taitung and Guangfu and Chihshang closer to Hualien. With the start of the Second World War, the sugar was more in demand than ever for converting to ethanol to meet Japan's fuel needs. A pineapple processing plant was also opened at Yuli. Not the least surprising aspect of traffic, reflected in the figures, was the volume of passengers. To better meet the needs of this, railcars were introduced from an early date, the first eight arriving from Nippon Sharyo in 1932. These were either petrol or gas powered but quickly proved successful, three more being supplied in both 1937 and 1939, also from Nippon Sharyo and with petrol/gas engines. In due course, all passenger services would be operated by railcars, with trailers added as necessary.

The introduction of railcars made a significant reduction in journey times possible, probably their main justification, but in the late 1930s the end to end journey between Hualien and Taitung typically still took between six and seven hours. Reflecting this, overnight services even included sleeping cars on some trains, rare but perhaps not unique for such a narrow gauge. They were certainly unique in their longevity, for a sleeping car service survived to the very end of 762mm gauge services in the early 1980s. Two third class examples survive today but to judge by the straight-backed wooden seats and hard wooden bunks, the spartan conditions were only for the most determined or adventurous traveller (although the bunks would provide considerably more space than an economy class seat on any of today's airlines).

In contrast to the major investment in new motive power for the sugar cane lines and some of the logging lines after the Chinese Nationalist occupation in 1945, the east coast line does not seem to have been a priority. A new bridge, some 2km long, had been built across the Mugua river south of Hualien in 1942, whether because of bombing, flooding or for another reason is not recorded.

Following Chiang Kai-shek's defeat in the Chinese civil war in 1949, around two million of his troops and supporters fled with him to Taiwan. Finding them homes and livelihoods was a matter of urgency and attention was given to opening up remote areas, including in some of the mountain areas, through construction of the first cross-island highway in the mid-1950s. With hindsight it seems surprising that more attention was not given at the time to upgrading the east coast line but presumably the south-east of the island was still considered remote and isolated.

Isolated and overlooked or not, traffic on the line grew steadily and quickly through the 1950s after a lull in the immediate aftermath of the ending of the war. In 1947 an average of 3835 passengers travelled on the line each day. By 1950 this had risen to 5385 and in 1958 to a peak for the decade of 13,377. Journeys were getting longer too, from an average of 30.4km in 1946 to 35.7km in 1960. Freight traffic grew similarly rapidly, from a daily average of just 192 tons in 1947 to 1324 a decade later. The main traffic was timber or timber related products: in the peak year of 1959 34,300 tons of cut logs and 90,000 tons of timber were carried and around 40,000 tons of sugar. In 1952 there were on average 54 trains daily on the line, or more than 19,000 annually. By 1957 that had risen to 89 daily and more than 32,000 per year. The entire line was operating at near full capacity and by the second half of the 1950s it was clear that expansion and upgrading was needed. The loco roster had benefited from new locomotives delivered during the war while the older locos continued to give good service so attention was first given to the passenger fleet. Some locally built railcars were added to the fleet and some of the surviving original railcars were rebuilt with diesel engines (a number were destroyed during Allied bombing of Hualien in the war). In this form they were to survive in use until the end of narrow gauge service.

Eventually, in the early 1960s, concerted thought finally seems to have been given to modernising the line, presumably once higher priorities elsewhere had been attended to and in recognition of continuing traffic growth. Starting in 1962, a series of 14 new railcars was delivered over the next eleven years, all with Cummins diesel engines and built either by the Tokyu Car Corporation in Japan or locally. With more powerful engines and much larger fuel tanks than previous models these were better suited to the long distances, and after the gauge was broadened in the 1980s most were converted to 1067mm gauge and saw several more years' service. Their introduction also saw a marked acceleration in timings, the fastest time for the end to end trip dropping to under 4 hours in 1966, over one-third less than the previous time.

The track was gradually upgraded and re-laid throughout with 22kg/metre rail, the same as used on the 1067mm gauge lines. This allowed the line speed limit to be raised to 70km/hour and by 1969 there were three expresses daily in each direction, making the journey in 3 hr 10 minutes including seven intermediate stops, at an average speed of just under 54km/hr. There were nine further passenger trains over the whole line in each direction, including the sleeping car service, a train typically being one railcar pulling one or two trailers. There were a further 16 short distance passenger workings in each direction and almost as many freight workings, the traffic being mainly sugar, forest and agricultural products. The line was still single track with passing loops, worked on the absolute block and tablet system.

Despite the upgrades to services by the 1970s, as one of the original 'Asian Tigers', Taiwan was changing rapidly and the line was clearly inadequate to meet modern needs. On 1st February 1980 Hualien was finally connected to the main Taiwan Railways Administration network with completion of the 1067mm gauge North Link line from Suao. By then the decision had already been taken to convert the line between Hualien and Taitung to the same gauge but the project awaited completion of the line to the north. Thereafter work proceeded quickly in two stages. The first section of converted line opened in 1981 and the remainder in June 1982.

Although the new 1067mm gauge line used the track bed of the original for much of the way, the opportunity was taken to improve the alignment for higher speeds wherever suitable. This included the construction of at least five tunnels, among them an under-river tunnel at Hsikou to replace the former zig-zag and bridge that was vulnerable to flooding. For some years after the conversion, many of the original stations remained, albeit adapted or modernised over the years and in places the old track bed was also clearly visible from passing trains. Inevitably, however, with the passage of time such remains have steadily disappeared. Most stations have now

LDK57, Kisha Seizo Kaisha works no. 544 of 1921, waits to cross a train, March 1966. The loco survives today as a static exhibit in Japan.

M Umemura

been rebuilt completely to comply with latest accessibility and safety standards while the line has been progressively upgraded and electrified and is currently in the course of being doubled throughout. A casual visitor today could be forgiven for not realising that a narrow gauge line had once passed this way.

Motive power

As might be expected, to begin with the separate companies followed their own policies in motive power, reflecting their own needs and traffic expectations. On the northern line between Hualien and Yuli, the first locomotives recorded in the roster were supplied by Andrew Barclay. The order for them was reportedly placed in 1911 but they did not arrive until much later, bearing works numbers 1342 and 1343 of 1915, both 14.25 ton 0-6-0Ts, very similar in design to the earlier locos supplied by the same builder for the Alishan line, the most immediately obvious difference being the spark arresters fitted to the latter. By the time they arrived at Hualien, four 0-6-0Ts from Vulcan Iron Works in the USA had already been delivered and the Barclays were initially given line running numbers 5 and 6. The Vulcans were works numbers 1457 and 1458 of 1910 and 1671 and 1672 of 1911, just under 14 tons in weight. At least two and possibly three of them had seen prior use on the Alishan railway before coming to the east coast.

These locomotives may always have been intended primarily for the initial construction rather than full operations, for in 1913 the northern line placed an order

Serving a remote and underdeveloped area, in its early years at least the east coast line was not unlike many of the Irish narrow gauge lines, or those in parts of France. Most of the passenger traffic could be handled comfortably by railcars, augmented as necessary by trailers, as in this March 1966 photo of a typical passenger train approaching Taoyeh (now Luye) near the summit of the line and not far from Taitung. These early railcars were re-engined after the Second World War and remained in use until the line was re-gauged.

M Umemura

for three rather larger 21.6 ton 0-8-0Ts from H K Porter. Bearing works numbers 5644-6 these were delivered in 1915 and were to remain in service for over fifty years, only being withdrawn in 1969 when most steam working ended. The design was clearly deemed satisfactory for a further five 0-8-0Ts, to similar overall specifications in terms of axle weight and tractive effort, were ordered between 1917 and 1923, this time from Japanese makers, four from the Osaka works of Kisha Seizo Kaisha and one from Nippon Sharyo. They were subsequently followed by similar locomotives to the same design from the same builders and also from Hitachi, a total of thirteen such being supplied up to 1938. They proved long-lived, all remaining in service until the end of most steam working in 1969 and two lasting as station pilots at Hualien and Taitung to the very end of 762mm operations in 1982. Meanwhile one more 0-6-0T was delivered, again from Japan, Nippon Sharyo works no 195 arriving in 1928.

The first locomotive on the southern line was also a Porter and another 0-6-0T, this time of 11 tons, works number 5616 of November 1914. If its proximity and similarity to the order for the northern line suggests an element of co-operation, the next two locos indicate otherwise and appear to have been acquired second hand, suggesting a degree of frugality on the part of the Taitung management or that capital was harder to come by. Both were 0-6-0Ts. No. 2 was a 12 ton Baldwin, presumably acquired from one or other of the sugar mill lines, joined in 1918 by a slightly larger Orenstein & Koppel 0-6-0T of 15.4 tons, probably works number 5808, one of a batch of seven built in 1912 for the Imperial Government Railway in Japan, where it carried the running number 204. They were followed in 1920 by another new Porter, works number 6520, this time an 0-4-0T.[*] Upon completion of the whole line between Hualien and Taitung, the loco fleet was re-numbered and consolidated. With the exception of O&K 5808 which remained in service until the end of general steam working in 1969 and has since been preserved, all the other locos from the southern line were withdrawn around this time, none surviving to be recorded in the renumbered fleet. Some of them may have remained in service under different management at Hualien and Taitung ports, or gone to sugar mills.

The stock was again re-numbered in 1937 following formal absorption into the government railway system, and in line with its practice all numbers received the letter 'L' as a prefix, for 'light' (i.e. narrow gauge), followed in French style by a letter indicating the number of driving axles, either 'C' or 'D'. At this time, when it was at its pre-war peak, there were 21 locos on the roster, eight 0-6-0Ts and the remainder 0-8-0Ts. The fleet would be renumbered once more in 1946 following the Chinese takeover, this time acquiring an additional letter, either 'K' to indicate a tank loco or 'T' for tender. Thus, the Andrew Barclay which first carried the number 5 then L10 upon the first re-numbering in 1928 became LC101 in 1937 and survived to be re-numbered yet gain as LCK10 in 1946.

Two more 0-6-0Ts were ordered in 1941 presumably to help with shunting and local requirements. Reflecting the general wartime demands on major manufacturers these came from a small Japanese builder, Kataoka Ironworks (片岡鉄工所) and appear to have been its only deliveries to Taiwan. Japanese sources record them as entering service in 1941 but Taiwanese ones two years later.

The preference for locos with neither leading nor trailing axles on what was a relatively long line may seem unusual but end to end traffic was limited, most of it being confined to shorter journeys to or from the harbours at either end. Operations were handled accordingly. Most trains, whether freight or passenger, were short trip workings over only part of the line. Through trains were few and through working of locomotives over the whole line uncommon. The prevalence of railcars for passenger workings may also have been a factor. A large loco shed and servicing facility were constructed at Yuli and most trains appear to have worked either north or south from there. But change came in 1941 when the line received its first and only tender locomotives, and its first with leading or trailing axles, in the form of four 2-8-2s from Nippon Sharyo. These were of that builder's KK900 class, originally designed for the government-owned narrow gauge railways in Korea. Weighing 56 tons including tender, they were more than twice the weight of the largest 0-8-0Ts and boasted a tractive effort almost 70% greater. They seemed ideal for the heavy traffic of wartime conditions and indeed for working over the full length of the line.

The class saw many years' service in Korea, seeing out steam operations on South Korea's last two narrow gauge lines between Suwon and Yeoju and Incheon in the 1970s. The last four remained in store in the shed at Suwon until the site was cleared for redevelopment in the early 1980s. All have survived as static exhibits, one of them at the Korean Railway Museum. At least one 762mm gauge steam loco also survived

---

[*] The government records for 1922 show the southern line as having just three locomotives, all Baldwins, which I ascribe to an error in transcription

An early train on the northern line between Hualien and Yuli behind one of the Vulcan 0-6-0Ts. Many of the passengers appear to be aborigines, possibly a consequence of police action.

Taipics.com

in North Korea until 2006. Although described as a 2-8-0, it is not clear whether this too was originally of the same class. In Taiwan, they were certainly a step-up from the existing loco fleet for as well as their size and apparent capability they were also the only superheated locos on the line. But in contrast to Korea, they do not appear to have been as successful or popular as the tank locomotives they were presumably intended eventually to replace, although the rapidly growing traffic of the 1950s and early 1960s meant they remained in service until the introduction of diesels in 1968. Two more members of the class were apparently destined for Taiwan but the ship carrying them sank *en route* and while one replacement was ordered, it ended up being sent instead to Korea.

In contrast to the 1067mm lines, upon which diesel traction was introduced gradually, in part because of a strategic decision to electrify the entire main line between Taipei and Kaohsiung which was completed in the early 1980s, on the Huatung line dieselisation was rapid and comprehensive. In November 1968 the first of twelve B-B diesel hydraulic centre cab locos were delivered from Nippon Sharyo. Designated LDH ('Light Diesel Hydraulic') these appear to have been standard 1067mm gauge locos running on narrower bogies for photographs show them overhanging the track significantly. This was probably intentional, for after the line was converted to 1067mm gauge, they were all converted too and continued to provide several more years' service. They were followed soon after by a locally built centre-cab, also a B-B diesel hydraulic but with a lower power rating so presumably intended mainly for shunting.

Once all the Nippon Sharyo diesels were delivered, steam working came to a rapid end, finishing formally in October 1969. Most of the steam fleet could be seen dumped at Hualien and Yuli in the early 1970s awaiting disposal. The only exceptions were two of the early 0-8-0Ts, Nippon Sharyo works number 81 of 1923 which survived as LDK58 and Hitachi works number 173 of 1925 which became LDK59 and which together remained as station pilots at Hualien and Taitung until the very end of services.

Although most of the line has been obliterated under subsequent development, the original terminus in Taitung survives as a heritage site, complete with station building, loco depot and other artefacts. The site of the original terminus in Hualien

1968 saw delivery of twelve of these B-B diesel hydraulics from Nippon Sharyo and the end of regular steam working over the main line. All twelve locos were re-gauged when the line was broadened in the 1980s and saw further use before being withdrawn. LDH203 is seen here at Yuli in March 1981 on a passenger train not long before the southern half of the line was widened to 1067mm.

Nicholas Pertwee

also survives. This is some 4km away from the new station which was built as part of the construction of the new line north in the 1980s. Although out of use since completion of gauge conversion in 1982, the original station technically remained open albeit inactive, until March 1988. After some years lying derelict it has now been transformed into a railway culture park. Several of the original office buildings have been restored and LDT103, the only remaining 2-8-2, is on static display on a short stretch of track here along with a couple of wagons and signals. O&K 5808, which became LCK 31 is on static display at a marble works north of Hualien. Four of the 0-8-0Ts also survive. The original numbers 22 and 23, Kisha Seizo Kaisha numbers 291 of 1918 and 544 of 1921, which became LDK56 and LDK57 respectively, were shipped to Japan where they became static exhibits. LDK 58 and LDK 59 remained with the TRA. LDK58 has been externally restored and is now on display outside Taipei railway station, together with one of the railcars. LDK59 meanwhile has been restored to full working order. After gauge conversion, a short stretch of 762 mm gauge track remained in the goods yard at Hualien. This has been extended to a length of around 900 metres and a new shed built where the loco is kept, together with a railcar and two trailers, including one of the sleeping cars. Although in full working order, it is steamed only rarely so seeing it in action is largely a matter of good fortune.

Despite dieselisation, two of the 0-8-0Ts remained in service as station pilots, one each at Hualien and Taitung, until the very end of narrow gauge services in the early 1980s. LDK58 is seen here at Hualien shunting empty coaching stock in March 1981, just months before the end of narrow gauge services.

Nicholas Pertwee

Until the confusion surrounding its origin can be cleared up, it is also possible that the Nippon Sharyo tank currently on static display at the Chihnan Forest Park near Hualien is LCK42 (see the text box in Chapter 4). The locally built diesel hydraulic is on static display together with another railcar in the railway park at Miaoli, on the west side of the island.

East Coast logging lines

In addition to the major forest reserves at Alishan and Pahsienshan on the western side of Taiwan's Central Mountain Range and Taipingshan to the north east, three smaller reserves with potential for exploitation were identified on the east coast, at Lanshan (嵐山), Muguashan (木瓜山) or Chihnan, and Lintianshan (林田山) or Morisaka. These lie close to one another in an arc from north-west to south-west around the city of Hualien. All three had rail connections to the east coast railway, development of which in turn facilitated exploitation of the timber reserves. Stands of cypress trees made Lintianshan especially attractive. Operations at all three sites were in the now customary pattern of quasi-private public ownership. At both Lintianshan and Muguashan and probably Lanshan too, this was by the Hualien Port Development

One that got away. In addition to the 12 diesels from Nippon Sharyo, a further one for service on the 762mm gauge was built locally, entering service in 1970. This one was not re-gauged however, and was withdrawn from service when the line was broadened in the 1980s. It is now on display, together with some of the 762mm gauge railcars, at the Miaoli Railway park, where it was photographed on 15 November 2008.

Company and in later years all three were to be under combined management of the Muguashan region of the Forestry Bureau.

Lintianshan was the first area to be exploited. As at Pahsienshan and Taipingshan, initial access was possible via a river valley and in 1918 a 32km long railway line was built along this from Pinglin (later Fenglin), a station on the east coast railway. Like the early lines at Taipingshan, this appears to have been powered by a combination of human effort and gravity. Over 9,000m³ of timber was brought out along this line before operations were suspended in 1934. For what reason is not entirely clear – the company may have lacked capital, or may have exhausted the more readily accessible stands of timber and simply decided that it was not cost effective to try to exploit other areas.

Then in 1939 the reserve was taken over by the Taiwan Xingye Company, which operated the paper mill at Lotung, the main customer for timber from Taipingshan. It also opened a new pulp mill south of Hualien, with a rail connection to the east coast line, so timber from all three reserves could be brought direct by train without any need for transhipment. Following the Chinese takeover in 1945, the Xingye company was nationalised (its name notwithstanding, it was Japanese registered and relied mainly on Japanese capital) as the Chung Hsing Paper Corporation. Operations carried on much as previously.

LDK58 as it is today. After some years as a static exhibit on Penghu (the Pescadores) and corrosion in the salt-laden air, it was returned to Taiwan, restored in TRA's works and is now a static exhibit outside Taipei Main Station, together with railcar LDR2201 from 1957. 30 May 2016.

On takeover in 1939, the company set about developing a major forestry centre at Lintianshan, approximately three kilometres up the valley from the east coast railway, to which a new rail connection was provided some way to the south of the original link at what is now Wanrong. It is possible that loco LC101, originally no 5 of the east coast line, Andrew Barclay 1342 of 1915, was leased or lent to the company to work this link almost from the outset in 1940. What is certain is that by 1951, now re-numbered as LCK10, it had been formally transferred and spent the remainder of its working life on this short link, eventually being withdrawn in 1962.

Forestry Bureau accounts say it was joined in the later 1950s by a 'similar' loco built by the Taiwan Machinery Company. While possible, there does not appear to be any separate corroboration for this and Transport Ministry statistics record just one steam locomotive on the line in 1962. But considering it together with the confusion surrounding locomotives on the Lotung Forestry Railway in the late 1950s, a plausible hypothesis might be that the Forestry Bureau took delivery of several locomotives from the Taiwan Machinery Co., which were then allocated amongst its various lines without a clear record being kept of which locos went to which particular line. If any such locomotive was sent to Lintianshan, its working time there must have been short-lived, for by the mid-1960s a Kato tractor had taken over responsibility for working the link to Wanrong.

Beyond the main logging centre, access to the forests was by the familiar combination of logging lines and two lengthy cableways which together took the line up to a height of 2600 metres. These lines eventually extended for around 25km. The Port Development Company may have already introduced mechanical power before ceasing operations, for the 1947 records show locos no 1 and 8 as four cylinder 27hp.

LDT103, the only survivor of the four Nippon Sharyo 2-8-2s, on display at Hualien Railway Culture Park, 6 August 2016.

5 ton Kato tractors built in 1928. At the time, they were accompanied by four other tractors, all 5 ton Katos, three of them 6 cylinder 35hp. models from 1942 and a single eight cylinder, 60 hp. model from 1938. All of them were powered by charcoal gas and had a top speed of 15 kph. Charcoal was readily accessible in Taiwan from the plentiful timber supplies and labour was cheap, so the cost of first making charcoal, then firing it up for long enough to produce adequate gas, was not a factor. The probable working pattern for the locos of long periods of idleness followed by bursts of activity as a loaded train would be hauled to the nearest cableway also made this a practical fuel.

Kato also supplied two tractors to Taiwan in 1943 which may possibly have gone to Lintianshan and a further 5 in 1948/9, all 5 ton and all recorded as gasoline powered (which could mean gas or petrol), one or more of which might similarly have gone there. By 1962, when steam working on the Wanrong spur ended, there were 9 loco-tractors in use, all of them either petrol or diesel-powered, the last five charcoal gas-powered examples having been fitted with diesel engines the previous year. Logging continued at Lintianshan until 1987 but rail operations ended in 1979, when completion of a road led to trucks taking over the traffic.

Construction of a railway and associated ropeways started at Muguashan in 1930, and Lanshan around the same time. By 1939 four of the five ropeways plus around 90% of the principal logging line at Muguashan were complete. The railway here

When the 1067mm gauge North Link line was opened in the early 1980s, a new through station was built on the western side of Hualien town centre and the old 762mm gauge station near the harbour was closed. After lying disused for some years, part of the site has now been restored and preserved as a Railway Culture Park, with old artefacts, including rolling stock and LDT103, on display. This view, looking west towards the mountains, is on the alignment of the original line, 6 August 2016.

Lintianshan today, a preserved Kato tractor and single carriage, latterly used on shuttle services to and from the TRA line at Wanrong, on display in the complex, 5 August 2016.

was interconnected by five ropeways whose combined length was 4.7km. The first section alone was just under 1.5km long, with a vertical rise of 687 metres. With the installation of the fifth and final ropeway in 1964, the railway extended to just short of 50km. Taking into account the relative remoteness of Hualien, still without a rail link to the rest of the country at the time, this must have made it the most isolated and remote of all the logging lines in the country.

As at Lintianshan to the south, the main wood sorting centre was some way from the junction with the east coast line and there are local accounts of American steam locomotives being used on this section. Like the Andrew Barclay tank locos, the four original Vulcan Iron Works 0-6-0Ts on the east coast line survived to be re-numbered as TRA locos in 1947 before being withdrawn, so it is quite possible that one or more of them ended its days at Muguashan in much the same way as the Barclay at Lintianshan. Government statistics for 1950 suggest there were as many as 8 steam locomotives at Muguashan although this number is more likely to refer to the whole region, so including Lintianshan and Lanshan. It still seems a surprising number as weight restrictions on the ropeways and the fire risk would preclude their use on anything other than connecting spurs or shunting work in the yards. It is not impossible that one or more of the Lotung Forestry Railway locos

Lintianshan: the railway followed the course of the river along its right bank for several kilometres before reaching the first aerial ropeway, 5 August 2016.

may have been transferred here in the 1950s although given its own needs this seems unlikely.

Otherwise, this was once more the domain of Kato rail tractors. One of the 4.5 ton 50hp 1951 deliveries is on display at the Chihnan Forest Park today, so presumably some others too of this order made their way to the reserve. It is described as 'fuelled by gasoline' (not charcoal gas) and capable of pulling 10 loaded cars or 40 tons. Central records mention 5 locos (other than steam) on the line in 1950, 12 by 1960 when the system was near its full extent and 22 in total on the three systems at Muguashan, Lanshan and Lintianshan in 1970. Muguashan also holds the double distinction of having the last working logging ropeway, which ceased operations in 1987 and of receiving the last new locos delivered for forestry use in the country. With the 1951 Katos ageing, a small number of new industrial diesels were delivered from Schoema in West Germany in 1972. Some of the Katos continued in use until 1980, while the Schoemas saw out the end of logging at Muguashan in 1989, the very last logging railway in Taiwan. All commercial logging in the country ended two years later.

The first of the east coast reserves to end logging was that at Lanshan, despite it being the last to see major expansion. Three new branches were added to the system

A rebuilt ropeway pylon with workmen's carriage underneath, Chihnan Forest Park, 6 August 2016.

in the late 1950s to exploit even more remote timber and a fourth and final one as late as 1971. It closed upon completion of the new TRA east coast line in 1982. Of the three, it is also the one about which least is known, despite being the most extensive, possibly and somewhat ironically because of its location. Lintianshan was sufficiently far from any centre of population for the pulp mill to develop a self-contained village for forestry workers on site. This survives today as a museum and local cultural centre. A Kato tractor and workmen's carriage have been preserved on site and a short stretch of track on a trestle has been rebuilt. Two of the Katos previously used here have also been preserved in private ownership nearby.

At Muguashan the local government has developed the Chihnan Forest Park as a small resort-cum-educational centre. It is attractively laid out, with forest walks in the vicinity and some of the old equipment preserved, as at Lintianshan. This includes the winding mechanism of one of the aerial ropeways and a section of ropeway complete with passenger carrying vehicle for workmen underneath, as well as the ubiquitous Kato. Also on display here, unfortunately in poor condition, are 18 ton Shay no 16 from the Alishan Forest Railway and a Nippon Sharyo loco, wrongly identified as an Andrew Barclay loco, and thought to have come from the Lotung Forestry Railway (see chapter 4). A short, 200 metre section of track has also been turned into an 'amusement railway' aimed at children on which a Schoema diesel previously hauled

And the real thing – a photo from a display board at Lintianshan. Note the baby being carried by the workman on the extreme right!

Taiwan Forestry Bureau

a short train of two four wheel Decauville style open side toast rack carriages. At the time of writing (2016) this appeared to have been out of action for some years with no plans to restore it to working order. Hualien city is however reportedly undertaking a feasibility study for installing a tourist cable-car line on the site of the first ropeway at Muguashan.

By contrast, the lower end of the Lanshan system has been swallowed up in the development of Hualien city and all trace has disappeared. Much of the track and supporting trestles remain *in situ* in the mountains however, slowly decaying. The area is officially closed on safety grounds although the remains can still be explored by the intrepid. A series of clips on YouTube shows both what is left and the care and precautions needed to explore. There are also two splendid films on YouTube showing latter day operations at Lanshan and Muguashan respectively, both of which convey the drama not only of the ropeways but also of the rail operations clinging to the precipitous mountainsides.*

* https://www.youtube.com/watch?v=FYOn08zXhfM (retrieved 29 June 2015);
  https://www.youtube.com/watch?v=UYxwIKMz8BA;
  https://www.youtube.com/watch?v=w_Zqx5pr3NA (retrieved 29 June 2015)

6

COPPER, COAL AND CROWDS:
LAST LINES AROUND TAIPEI

Wudu and the coast

At first glance, a passenger today on a train passing through Wudu station in Taipei's eastern suburbs would see nothing remarkable about the area. Blocks of flats indicate its status as a pleasant residential commuter district. The adjacent landscaped banks of the Keelung River with their cycleways give no hint of the town's industrial past. But the observant traveller, looking backwards over his or her left shoulder on entering the station on a Keelung bound train will notice a strangely decorated waterworks on the far side of the river. A closer look will show the decoration to be photo-murals of steam hauled narrow gauge trains. These completely cover at least three walls of the waterworks and are the first and clearest hint of Wudu's past claim to fame as the home of three railways, on three gauges, using four different forms of motive power – but none of them electric.

Wudu owes this status primarily to a combination of geography and geology. In addition to timber, tea and sugar, Taiwan had been identified as holding significant mineral deposits, principally coal, sulphur and gold, all of which were particularly prominent in the very north of the island. Coal had been discovered in northern Taiwan in Chinese times. Significant deposits lay close to Keelung, the main harbour. These had a low ash content, making the coal highly desirable for steamships and the Chinese authorities developed a large mine to supply their Navy's southern squadron with most of its needs. Western navies and steamship companies were also aware of the deposits and keen to get access to them. After Keelung was opened to foreign vessels in 1860 as much as 18,000 tons annually was supplied to them but the mine was destroyed as a pre-emptive measure when the French shelled Keelung in 1884.

Other significant deposits were found south of Taipei, to the west around Yingge, which was to become the main source of coal for the government railways and to the east in the Pingxi valley, south east of Taipei. But the seams were mostly thin and fractured, rarely more than three feet thick, lying between sandstone strata and often steeply inclined. This made the coal expensive to mine and to the very end of coal-mining in Taiwan, the normal method was to dig an adit for as far as the incline and rock formation allowed before abandoning it. Despite this, local coal remained an important energy source into the 1950s and 1960s as Taiwan was anxious to retain a degree of energy security during the Cold War. What was a handicap for miners was to be a boon for railway enthusiasts. The oil price shocks of the 1970s gave the industry a further lease of life but cheaper foreign coal and then three major mining accidents in 1984 with over 250 fatalities led to the government closing most mines in 1985.

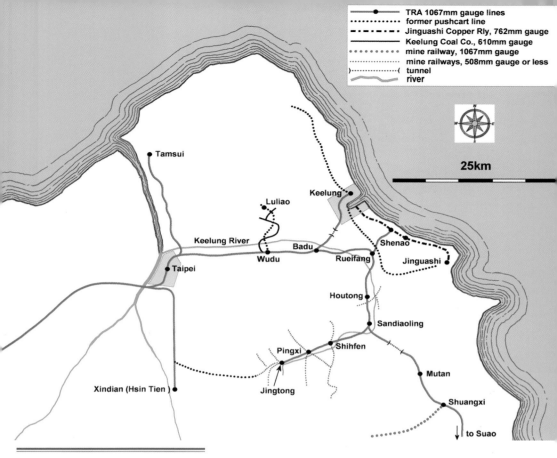

John Athersuch

For all the attractions of coal, it was gold that held the greatest initial appeal as the Japanese sought to open the island to development. Its presence too was known from Chinese times but once more production was on a cottage industry basis, mainly but not entirely through panning for alluvial gold. Unlike coal, which could be found all over the island, gold was found primarily in the north east, again close to Keelung, the Keelung River and its tributaries being the main focus of the panners. Japanese investors were keen to maximise the potential of the deposits and the Tanaka Company was quick to start developing a large mine at Kinkaseki or Jinguashi (金瓜石) south east of Keelung. This was an isolated peak close by the sea, formed of hard igneous rock and rising to over 600 metres. The actual seams of gold were in the peak but the mill and other facilities were at sea level. This was one of the earliest major industrial complexes in Taiwan, employing more than 4000 people by 1903.

Ore was brought out of the mine on a tramway, then to the mill by aerial ropeway and after processing was initially shipped to Keelung on a push-cart line for export. For all the early promise, however, it was copper rather than gold that was to be the long-term attraction of the mine.

Whether the Tanaka company went bankrupt, or for some other reason is not clear but in due course the mine was taken over by the Japan Copper Company and

An undated postcard showing an almost certainly posed view of a train on the Jinguashi line behind one of its three Nippon Sharyo locomotives.

National Central Library of Taiwan

re-opened in August 1930 primarily as a copper mine although gold continued to be recovered. Copper was in growing demand for the Japanese economy and the existing push-cart line, which also had at least two inclines *en route*, presumably cable-worked, would have been quite inadequate for shipping the ore to the harbour. Furthermore, with gold and copper increasingly being mined at different levels within the mountain, direct access to the seams was ideally required, rather than having all the ore first shipped to the mill. In 1919 a big hydro-electric project at Sun Moon Lake in the centre of Taiwan had been developed. To help with its construction an electric tramway had been built and thought was given to providing a similar line at Jinguashi. Possibly because of positive experience on the logging lines, however, the decision was eventually taken to construct a conventional 762mm gauge line, using internal combustion from the outset. This provided direct rail access to three levels of the mine, in itself no small achievement and a direct, 12.2km route to Keelung harbour, a combination of tunnels and viaducts replacing the former inclines.

The line opened in 1936, with three 0-4-0 internal combustion locos from Nippon Sharyo as the motive power. Although primarily an industrial line, carrying ore and metals to the port, a passenger service was also provided, whether for the public or for workers only is not clear. The mine remained in production until 1986 but the railway was abandoned in 1962. In 1965 however a thermal power station was built at Shen Ao, roughly midway along the line. The TRA built a new branch from Ruifang on its main line as far as Shen Ao to deliver coal to the power station. Having done so, it

The Keelung Coal Company's 610mm gauge line was the last industrial narrow gauge operation in Taiwan using steam power. Based in the Taipei suburbs, it brought coal to an interchange point with the TRA at Wudu, using a series of 3 ton and 5 ton well tank locos for its services. In this 1972 scene, a 3 ton loco is on the left and a 5 ton one on the right at the line's shed.

Kurashige Nobutaka

also took over the part of the old 762mm line east of Shen Ao, re-gauged it to 1067mm and re-opened it in 1969 for both freight and passengers. In this form, it lasted until 1989 when road competition finally put paid to it. Part of the line remained in use for coal trains to and from the power station at Shen Ao until this was decommissioned in 2007. A short, 4.2km stretch was re-opened for passengers in 2014 but this is not on the original section of narrow gauge line.

In contrast to the industrial scale of the Jinguashi copper mine and with the exception of the government owned mine at Keelung, the early coal mines were almost always small in scale. The output of individual mines was rarely large enough to justify a dedicated branch line off the government network, even where geography would have permitted this, nor even for the mine to have its own network. In most cases the smaller gauge lines built into the adits themselves to bring out the coal were simply extended to a point where coal could be transhipped on to the government railway. This could be a matter of a hundred or so metres or it could be a couple of kilometres although longer distances usually justified building a separate line to the transhipment point. The mines were developed by private enterprise with each company free to choose whatever gauge and type of motive power would suit it best. The result was a complex of narrow gauge lines on a variety of different gauges and using at least three distinct types of motive power – conventional locomotives, cable haulage and human power.

One of the Keelung Coal Co.'s 5 ton locos hauling a rake of empties back to the mine. A carriage for workmen is at the back of the train.

Kurashige Nobutaka

Many of the last lines have already been described by Charles Small, whose photographs and descriptions in *Rails to the Mines* wonderfully capture their charm and idiosyncracies. Especially notable is a journey he took on the 610mm line of the Keelung Coal Company in 1972, during which the train came off the rails and his camera was broken. A happier consequence was that in trying to get back to Taipei from the wreck, he discovered the Yourui (友蚋) push-cart line, which he also describes.* Still using human power, this line included a tunnel, a double track section with a junction complete with diamond crossing, banker duties on the steepest grades and for good measure regular passenger trains. Sadly, both systems have now gone. The Yourui line was the last traditional push-cart line in the country, lasting until 1976. In May the following year the Keelung coal company line, the last 610mm gauge line in the country, followed it into oblivion. These two lines both started from Wudu, across the river from the TRA station and are the ones referred to at the start of the chapter. The waterworks at Wudu was built on the site of the Keelung coal line's depot, from where a connection was provided to the TRA sidings by a cable-worked stretch of line across a suspension bridge (by the time these lines closed, diesel power was in increasing use on the TRA lines through Wudu and this is the fourth form of motive power referred to). Other than some bridge piers a few kilometres away, the photo murals provide the only evidence that there was once a narrow gauge line here.

---

* Small calls this the Yuna line but all maps and signs in the area refer to the locality as Yourui (*pinyin*) or Youruei.

By 1972 a weak bridge towards the upper end of the line meant that the heavier 5 ton locos were confined to the lower section and trains changed locomotives at Yourui, the mid-point, even though the line was only about 5km long in total. By this time, it also appears to have been down to just two serviceable locos. Here, the 5 ton loco has just arrived with empties on the left hand track and will shortly reverse roles with the smaller loco on the right and take over the loaded train and return with it to Wudu.

Kurashige Nobutaka

One might expect even less of the push-cart line to have survived. As it left Wudu, however, it passed a small coal mine at Dongshan (or Tungshan), also mentioned by Small. This closed in 1990 and most of the surface area has been transformed into an industrial estate but one small part has been kept as an open-air 'culture park', replete with replica push-cart and coal wagons. The tunnel on the line has been filled in but murals and an information board beside the road draw attention to the site of the former Yourui station, while a few kilometres up the valley, a short section of track with another replica push-cart marks the site of the old station at Luliao. The bridge which took the line under the Taipei-Keelung motorway also survives although there is nothing to indicate that a push-cart line once passed through it. Happily, both lines survived long enough to be recorded on film and clips of both in action can be seen on YouTube.*

---

*   https://www.youtube.com/watch?v=tDsQtkaZ3xE (retrieved 13 July 2015);
https://www.youtube.com/watch?v=C8q43qzFJR4.
The same Japanese site, Kuroganerail, also has some wonderfully atmospheric photographs of the line in its last days: http://www.kurogane-rail.jp/jinsha/ejs29.html (both retrieved 5 October 2016)

The coal loading facility at the mine in 1976. Not too much evidence of health and safety regulations!
Nicholas Pertwee

Motive power on the Yourui line was human, usually male for freight 'trains' and female for passengers and as bankers. On the Keelung coal railway, it was several Japanese built 0-4-0Ts of two different sizes, the smaller ones weighing 3.5 tons and the larger ones 5 tons. Small says these were originally used for the building of an airfield at Kaohsiung from where they were acquired second hand in the late 1940s. 610mm was apparently the preferred gauge of the Japanese Navy so if it was a naval airfield this is plausible. But Taiwanese sources suggest the locos were acquired new, at different times between 1936 and 1941. Following closure at least three of the locos found their way back to Japan. No. 3, built in Osaka in 1936, was sold to Japan in 1971 before the line closed and was followed in 1978, shortly after closure, by no 6, also of 3.5 tons and built in Osaka and originally acquired in 1941. Both are now in use at a children's farm near Tokyo's Narita airport. The frame of one of the larger locos is also reported to be there.

The Pingxi valley

The greatest concentration of coal mines in the country was in the Pingxi (or Pinghsi – 平溪) valley, south east of Taipei. Some of these were also to be the last operational coal mines in Taiwan. The valley is narrow and mountains rise steeply on either side of the river making it difficult to penetrate. But coal seams abound, especially around Jingtong, towards the western or upper end of the valley. Exploitation of them started

By 1976 when Nicholas Pertwee visited the Keelung line the stock had definitely seen better days. Here one of the 5 tonners is prepared for another turn of duty.

Nicholas Pertwee

The 3 ton locos faced chimney first towards the mine and the 5 tonners the other way round, indicating that this particular loaded train is on the upper section of the line, behind the last serviceable 3 tonner, March 1976.

Nicholas Pertwee

Both the Keelung Coal Co. and Yourui push-cart lines terminated across the river from the TRA station at Wudu with separate suspension bridges from both lines providing access to the transhipment sidings, the former using cable haulage and the latter human power. Although the Yourui line had closed by the time this photo was taken in 1977, the bridge remained in use to bring coal from the Tungshan mine, just across the river.

John Tillman

soon after the Japanese occupation, access at first being by a push-cart line from the west. This required a long gradient up to the pass at the top of the valley, the only mitigating factor being that loaded carts had the benefit of the downhill slope. Then in 1921 private interests built a 1067mm gauge line up the valley from a junction on the recently completed government railway around the north coast. This provided much improved access and further investment in the mines at Jingtong followed.

In due course, the six separate seams here were to be joined by an extensive 495mm gauge rail network. Much of this was underground, probably the only place in Taiwan where separate mine seams were linked in this way. But reflecting the geography of the valley, some of the lines were on the surface, including two lengthy cable-worked inclines, one up to the mine at the top of the valley which had first been linked by the push-cart line from Xindian. This network took coal from all the seams to a central washery and transfer point to the 1067mm line at Jingtong station. This remained the principal coal loading point on the line for many years although the small and scattered nature of the mines meant that coal was also loaded at other points along the valley, usually from a small loading hopper at an individual siding. Much later, the development of mines around Shihfen, roughly half way along the valley, meant that it became a second focal point for transhipping coal. The village of Shihfen itself was built along either side of the railway and the line still runs down the main street today.

Not quite what it seems. This photo of a Keelung Coal company train crossing the Yourui stream covers a wall of the Wudu waterworks. 7 May 2016.

The Keelung Coal company at Wudu ceased operations in the 1970s but mining in the Pingxi valley was to continue for another twenty years until 1997. While most mines had been forced to shut in 1985, an exception was made for a small number of mines, partly because the government was anxious to protect jobs but also because they included some newer mines with higher standards of safety. The few remaining mines finally succumbed to economics and a changing world in the final years of the twentieth century.

By the mid-1990s two clusters of mines were left, centred on Shihfen and Jingtong. Both boasted the newest mines. The Xipingxi mine at Shihfen was established as late as 1965 and started production two years later. According to a British enthusiast who visited in November 1993, one of the small mines at Jingtong was even newer. Only the Xipingxi mine was of any size and by this date most remaining mines were loading their coal directly into trucks using the road that now also runs along the valley. The mine rail systems were correspondingly short, often barely more than a hundred metres from mine entrance to loading point. By this late date too, most mines used cable haulage rather than brute force to bring the loaded tubs from mine to transfer point.

The Xipingxi mine, however, was about 1.2km from the TRA line and relied on a railway line to bring the coal out of the adits and down to the transfer point. The distance ruled out both cable and human haulage and instead the line used low voltage overhead electric power throughout, from the coal transfer hoppers at the

This mural beside the road between Wudu and Yourui is one of a number of reminders of the Yourui push-cart line, the last in the country. 9 June 2016.

Taiwan's last working coal mines were in the Pingxi valley, not far from Taipei. The very last mine in operation, the Xipingxi mine at Shihfen, was unusual in having a 495mm gauge overhead electric line linking the drift mine with the TRA exchange sidings to the south, using Japanese electric locomotives built in the 1930s.

John Raby

The Xipingxi mine closed in the late 1990s but survives today as a museum, complete with working railway, albeit now with battery electric power rather than overhead wires. Here a train returns visitors to the museum behind one of the original locos, now converted to battery operation. 11 November 2016.

TRA sidings right into the adits themselves. Although the mine was relatively new, the six four wheel locos that comprised the motive power were thought by one visitor to date from the 1930s, so presumably acquired second hand. Taiwanese sources state that the Taoyang mine at Jingtong once had similar locomotives so it is possible they came from there. They were all identical externally. Numbers 3 and 5 were built in Japan by Nichiyu (Nippon Conveyor Co.), No. 7 was also built in Japan by Hitachi and nos. 1, 2 and 6 in Taiwan, possibly on the basis of reverse engineering given their similarity to the Japanese locos. (As on other lines there was no number 4).

This mine was one of the very last to close, in 1997 when falling international coal prices made it uneconomic to continue. It reopened in 2002 as the Taiwan Coal Mine Museum, changing in 2012 to the Xipingxi Coal Mine Museum. At one time the access to the museum was by a footpath adjacent to the loading hoppers in the sidings close to TRA's Shihfen station. This structure has deteriorated badly over the years however and is now decaying and dangerous. A new road into the valley has been built in the meantime and access to the museum is now from a car park adjacent to the old adit. Both the railway line to the transfer sidings and all the locos remain intact. The masts for the overhead catenary also remain in situ although the overhead line itself has been removed. Most of the locos are now on static display only but two have been rebuilt with new motors powered by batteries. A highlight of a visit to the museum is a ride along the old line behind one of these locos in original coal tubs, modified only by the provision of crude plank seats and basic roofs. The loose couplings and absence of springs and continuous brakes make for an authentic if not entirely comfortable experience, notwithstanding the absence of overhead power.

An unrestored coal tub at the Xipingxi mining museum, showing clearly the wooden dumb buffers and basic construction, dating from the first push-cart lines in the country, 15 May 2016.

This system was built on the push-cart gauge of 495mm but lines at some other drift mines in the valley were reportedly on 508mm gauge, which was also used on industrial lines in the country. Just across the river from Shihfen were some more drift mines and as at Wudu on the Keelung system, cable haulage brought loaded coal tubs over suspension bridges to the 1067mm gauge sidings. This ended in 1991 when one of the suspension bridges collapsed. On the lines which did not use cable power, mainly further up the valley around Jingtong, modernisation was apparent in the form of basic internal combustion locomotives, usually using small single cylinder ChenYu diesel engines similar to those common on small agricultural tractors in the country. But the origins of all these lines in the Decauville principles of more than a century earlier were still apparent in single-bladed point work, the size and design of the coal tubs and above all in continued reliance on human power, especially for rudimentary but effective loading and unloading of wagons. One or two still boasted passenger trolleys. A flavour of these last lines can still be seen in a short clip on YouTube.[*] Thus a concept originally intended only for temporary use could still be seen in every day operation almost a century after its first introduction to Taiwan!

---

* https://www.youtube.com/watch?v=du-n0E3i648 (retrieved 13 July 2015)

Across the river to the south of Shihfen another, smaller mine remained in operation into the mid-1990s. Access to the TRA sidings was by a cable-worked line across this suspension bridge but when the bridge was declared unsafe in 1991, the railway closed, to be followed not long after by the mine itself.

John Raby

Wulai

Wulai lies a short distance south of Taipei city. High waterfalls, imposing mountain scenery and many hot springs combine to make it a popular weekend and day trip destination for Taipei residents and visitors alike. Access from the city is along a narrow river valley with steep, thickly forested mountains on either side. As explained in Chapter 2, the first attempts at development had been as early as 1904. Although unsuccessful, some short push-cart tracks were laid in connection with this and formed the genesis of subsequent development.

Then in 1921 the Mitsui Corporation was granted a licence by the government to start logging in the valley. Around the same time the privately-owned Taipei Railway Company (*Taihoku Tetsudo Kaisha*) started work on a 10.4km long 1067mm gauge railway to what is now the Taipei suburb of Xindian (Hsintien). This opened in 1922. Mitsui built a push-cart network starting from Xindian and running south along the valley towards Wulai and beyond to bring out the logs. By 1928 this reached Wulai itself and by the start of the Second World War it had become an extensive network of interconnected lines. Some were short – the shortest was only 500 metres – but the longest ran for 13km and the network continued some way beyond Wulai to Fushan, in aboriginal areas deep in the mountains.

By the early 1990s Taiwan was a prosperous middle-income country and its main line railway was fast approaching its centenary. But amazingly, last vestiges of the very early push-cart lines based on Decauville principles could still be found in the Pingxi valley. As well as the human motive power, the single-bladed pointwork that was typical of these lines can be clearly seen in this picture.

John Raby

Another type of pointwork, once common and still in use in 1993 was this blade-less type, where a successful change of direction was entirely down to the skill of the operator.

John Raby

Despite the hot springs, in Japanese times the area was designated as aboriginal land and access restricted. The restricted access policy was continued in the early years of Chinese Nationalist rule, indeed access to many mountain areas remained restricted into the 1990s in a legacy of this policy. A road had also been built to Wulai in the Japanese period. Although a bus service was operating along it from the 1930s, fuel shortages during and after the war prolonged service on the push-cart line into the 1950s. At some point thereafter the push-cart line between Xindian and Wulai was abandoned in favour of the road, together with the various branches constructed during the Mitsui era, leaving just the southernmost line from Wulai to Fushan. This eventually succumbed in 1963, by which year there were some 45km of push-cart lines still in use nationwide.

The road ended at the northern end of Wulai village which was in turn some 2km from the main waterfall. Wulai itself was the site of several hot springs and growing numbers of visitors were in the habit of using the push-carts to ride up the line to the waterfall, despite the official controls on access. With prosperity growing in the 1960s and the government keen to encourage tourism, the controls were finally relaxed and development of the area encouraged. When the remainder of the line closed in 1963, the short section from Wulai village to the falls was placed under local government management and new push-carts introduced. Built on steel frames, with padded seats and basic roofs these were a big step up from traditional push-carts

With its rudimentary and very basic looking civil engineering and permanent way, the Chungkuang mine system encapsulated the inherent charm of Taiwan's lesser narrow gauge lines right to the end of the 20th century.

John Raby

but still human powered. Traffic grew steadily and in 1974 the decision was taken to mechanise operations. The track was doubled, battery electric locomotive haulage was introduced and the original 'people power' became brakemen instead for the descent. The 1964 cars were still used, albeit improved with the addition of footrests and roll-down tarpaulins to provide further protection from the elements, often an issue in Taiwan. These cars were all single-ended, so time was lost, especially at busy periods, by the need to uncouple each one individually and turn it on a wagon turntable at each end of the line before every journey.

The Wulai area has continued to grow in popularity, especially at weekends, and to prevent the village and falls being overwhelmed by road traffic, the section of the valley from the north end of the village to south of the waterfall is closed to outside traffic, so visitors have the option of either walking or taking the train. Steady improvements have been made over the years to cope with the consequent growth, perhaps the most significant being the construction in 2002 of short tunnels and reverse loops at the termini to avoid the need for uncoupling and individual turning of carriages. At the same time the ten Japanese built battery electric power cars of 1974, each of which was capable of hauling two trailers, were replaced by diesel locos while the original push-carts have been succeeded by 4 seater carriages.

The Wulai line is now the only one in Taiwan on 545mm gauge. It is often assumed to be unique in this respect and generates discussion as to why this particular gauge

A locomotive and truck from the 508mm gauge Shuishan mine system, now on display at Jingtong station, terminus of the Pingxi valley line. 11 November 2016.

was chosen. It was certainly a less common gauge but as explained in Chapter 1 it was used on other push-cart lines, almost certainly including those of the Taichung Light Railway, so while unusual, the gauge is not unique. While the line's origins as a timber hauling push-cart tramway are all but unrecognisable in today's operations, a museum at the Falls end of the line gives a good history of the area and its development and includes a short demonstration stretch of push-cart line, complete with turntable. Unfortunately, in an all too common occurrence on Taiwan's railways, at the time of writing the line is not operating, several sections having been damaged in 2015 by two big typhoons in quick succession. Following repair work, the line re-opened in summer 2017.

Given the plethora of 'last lines' in the Taipei area it seems appropriate that apart from sugar lines, the last industrial narrow gauge line working in Taiwan was at a sand and silica mine in the Taipei suburbs, which closed in 2004. But this was not quite the end. Zhinan Temple, close to the zoo in Taipei's southern suburbs is one of the largest in the country and a popular spot to visit, especially at weekends and holidays. It even has its own station on the Maokong gondola line of Taipei's Rapid Transit system. The overwhelming majority of visitors come to enjoy the views over the city and the mountains, admire the statuary, pray or meditate, or to watch the puppet shows at the temple entrance. Few of them are likely to notice a rusty line of rails which descends steeply from the temple to the valley below. It is short – no more than 200 metres

The Wulai line re-opened in summer 2017 following repairs to weather damage sustained two years previously. A train is seen in action on 29 September 2017.

Last survivor. Wagons at the upper end of the Zhinan temple cable railway with the winding house behind. Note the single-bladed pointwork. 20 November 2016.

An ascending train on the Zhinan temple railway. Despite the concrete sleepers and steel framed wagons, Decauville concepts remain very much alive in the gauge and wagon design, more than 120 years after first being introduced to Taiwan. 20 November 2016.

— and almost completely obscured by overhanging trees. If they do, they could easily be forgiven for thinking it was long disused. But if they are fortunate they may see a couple of wagons descending or ascending slowly at the end of a cable. For this is still a working railway, cable-powered and used to bring supplies up to the temple. It has just three sidings, one of them now out of use. But with its 495mm gauge, Decauville inspired single-bladed point work and push-cart style wagons, historic influences from the very beginnings of Taiwan's narrow gauge are readily apparent and this short line can claim to be the last survivor in original form and purpose of a once-flourishing network.

Industrial narrow gauge may now be all but history, but Taiwan's remaining narrow gauge lines are busier than ever. Together with the many museums and historic sites around the country they provide a worthy and fitting testament to the island's rich and fascinating narrow gauge heritage. It is human nature to rue the 'ones that got away,' or for railway enthusiasts to pine over now lost lines they never managed to see while they were working. Sadly, most of Taiwan's lines fall well and truly into this category. But thanks to those in Taiwan who have done so much to protect and preserve what remains, future generations should still be able to appreciate something of the impact narrow gauge railways made in opening up and developing this enchanting country.

FURTHER READING AND BIBLIOGRAPHY

A considerable amount of information is available about the railways and associated industries in Taiwan, both in original records and published works, much of it accessible via the internet. Unfortunately for the western reader, most of it is in either Chinese or Japanese. For this reason, I have opted not to use footnotes other than for some specific quotes or matters of especial significance, reasoning that most of the references would be to works beyond the comprehension of most readers. I apologise if this causes any frustration but all the works I have drawn on or referred to in writing this book are listed below.

The Japanese colonial government in Taiwan helpfully recorded and published in Chinese much of the information it collected about the then province, including the annual statistical returns for the railways. These are a valuable source of basic information but need to be treated with some caution. At least until the end of the 1930s Chinese numerals and forms of measurement were still the norm for everyday use but the records use both Chinese and Arabic numbers, raising doubts about how accurately measurements were made and written down. Similarly, locomotive classes were frequently identified by a letter in Roman script to indicate the builder. But 'AB' (for Andrew Barclay) could be and was recorded as 'AD' while a 'V' for Vulcan often became an 'L' instead. Once such an error entered the records, it appears to have been carried over in future years rather than being corrected. The confusion arising from apparent errors in Forestry Bureau records is mentioned in the text.

The works lists of the different locomotive builders therefore provided an invaluable cross-reference and additional primary source. One limitation of these is that it was common for locomotives to be supplied to a trading agent acting on behalf of the end-user, rather than direct, so the works lists often simply record delivery to an agent, rather than the actual line for which a locomotive was destined. Deduction or guesswork is therefore still required to ascertain a specific end-user.

Much the best of the limited printed material in English about Taiwan's railways is that written by the late Charles Small. He included a chapter on Taiwan in *Rails to the Setting Sun* published in 1971. Although now somewhat dated this still offers an excellent introduction, while his later monograph of 1978, *Rails to the Mines,* remains the pre-eminent record in English of Taiwan's smaller industrial and push-cart lines. Both these are now long out of print. Small lived in Japan at the time he visited Taiwan and received advice and help from many Japanese enthusiasts, including a group known as Kemuri Pro who produced many hundreds of evocative photographs of Taiwanese narrow gauge lines in the 1960s, some of which Small published in his own books. The group produced just one book of their own, *Salute to Steam,* in 1971, copies of which are still readily available. Many more of their photographs are now being published by Nankaru Publishing in their series *Steam on 2ft. Tracks* which includes *Keelung 1966,* published in 2012. These are in Japanese only but the high quality photographs make accompanying text largely superfluous.

Loren Aandahl lived in Taiwan as a teenager in the 1960s. *The Taiwan Railway, 1966-1970* is his personal recollections of the railways in that period. Coverage is mainly of the TRA but includes a comprehensive chapter on the East Coast line and it is profusely illustrated. *Push Car Railways and Taiwan's Development* by Ronald Knapp in *China's Island Frontier, Studies in the Historical Geography of Taiwan,* which he edited (Honolulu 1980) gives a very good overview of the development of the push-cart lines, albeit from a mainly academic perspective. Taiwanese authors Hung Chih-wen (洪致文) and Su Chao Hsu (蘇昭旭) have produced several books on different aspects of Taiwan's railways. They are mainly written in Chinese although a book by Su on the Alishan railway is now available in English and some of Hung's include English summaries. But they are all profusely illustrated and convey a good flavour of the subject even for a non-Chinese reader.

More is available in digital form, especially via the web. For the general reader, an excellent introduction to Taiwan's railways is Su I-Jaw's ('Citycat') website, http://citycat.theweb.tw which is a treasure trove of photographs, old and not so old, of many of the different lines plus other valuable material, most of it with accompanying explanations in English as well as Chinese. Again, much has been made available by Japanese enthusiasts. Masaaki Umemura is a former member of the Kemuri Pro group and his site http://762mm.world.coocan.jp/sepiaironosyashintyou1.html has many superb photographs from a visit in 1966, some of which have been reprinted here. Another excellent site is www.kurogane-rail.jp; in particular N. Noguchi has posted some splendidly atmospheric photographs of the last days of steam on the sugar lines at http://www.kurogane-rail.jp/tsr/etsr_15.html. Other material available on kurogane-rail has been mentioned in specific footnotes.

Unless otherwise stated all the following material is published or recorded in the language first listed and English translations of titles are for guidance only

Primary Sources – government and other records

臺灣 鐵道要覽, 臺灣總督府鐵道部 (*Taiwan tiedaoyaolan, Taiwanzongdufu tiedaobu*) Review of Railway Operations, Railway Department of the Taiwan Governor General, various years, principally 1922, 1923 and 1931

中華民國交通年鑑, 交通部交通研究所編印 (*Zhonghua minguo jiaotongnianjian, jiaotongbu jiaotongyuanjiusuobianyin*) Republic of China Annual Review of Transport, Ministry of Transport Research Institute, various years between 1950 and 1975

臺灣省政府林產管理局印, 八仙山事業區施業案說明書,(*Taiwanshengzhengfulinchanguanlijuyin, Pahsienshanshiyequyeanshuomingshu*) Taiwan Provincial Government Forestry Bureau, Pahsienshan area explanatory report, 1953

臺灣省林務局, 八仙山事業區經營計劃 (*Taiwanshenglinwuju, Pahsienshanshiyequjingyingjihua*) Taiwan Provincial Government Forestry Bureau, Pahsienshan area management plan, 1967

Andrew Barclay – Locomotive Works Lists, Industrial Locomotive Society, http://www.industrial-loco.org.uk/works_list1200.htm, (retrieved 12 October 2016)

Nippon Sharyo Locomotive Works List

Other published works

The author's surname is listed first in all cases.

Aandahl, Loren: *The Taiwan Railway, 1966-1970,* Taiwan 2011

Chen Chia-hao (陳家豪): *Japanese Colonial Government, Local Economic Development and Taiwanese Capital: Taiwanese Push Car Railway (1903-1928),* in *Taiwan Historical Research,* vol 22, 2015 (in Chinese)

Council for Hakka Affairs: 林鐵尋跡：尋找消失的五分車，八仙山森林鐵路, (*Tracing the forest railway: looking for remains of the narrow gauge and Pahsienshan Forest railways*), Taipei 2009

Davidson, James: *The Island of Formosa Past and Present,* London 1903 (subsequently reprinted, including in modern facsimile versions)

Far Eastern Review, various years from 1908

Fricke, Klaus, Bude, Roland, Murray, Martin: *Orenstein & Koppel: O&K Steam Locomotives Works List, 1892-1945,* Bristol 1978

Hung Chih-wen (洪致文): *A Century Rolling: Taiwan Railways,* Taipei 2015 (in Chinese with English summaries)

Hung Chih-wen (洪致文): 台灣火車的故事 (*Taiwan huochede gushi – The story of Taiwan's trains*), Taipei 1993

Hung Chih-wen (洪致文): 臺灣火車的故事 – *Taiwan railway story and sugar cane railway sl,* Taipei 1993 (in Chinese)

Kent, P.H: *Railway Enterprise in China, An Account of its Origin and Development,* London 1907

Knapp, Ronald G: *Push Car Railways and Taiwan's Development* in Ronald G. Knapp ed.: *China's Island Frontier, Studies in the Historical Geography of Taiwan,* Honolulu, 1980

Lin Hong-Chung (林鴻忠) ed.: 太平山古往今來 ： 林業歷史 (*Taipingshan Past to Present*), Taiwan 2007

Lin Qing Chi (林清池): 太平山開發史 (*Taipingshan Kaifanshi – History of Taipingshan Development*), Taipei 1996

Okamoto, Noriyuki (岡本-憲之): 加藤製作所 機関車図鑑 (Kato Works' Locomotives), Tokyo 2014

Okita, Yusaku (沖田祐作): 機関車表 (Kikansha Hyo – Locomotive List), Tokyo 2014

Small, Charles S: *Rails to the Setting Sun,* Tokyo, 1971

Small, Charles S: *Rails to the Mines: Taiwan's Forgotten Railways,* Honolulu 1978

Small, Charles S: *Far Wheels II,* USA 1986

Su Chao Hsu (蘇昭旭): 台灣鐵路車站圖誌 (*Taiwan tielu chezhan tuzhi – Taiwan Railway station records*), Taipei 2002

Su Chao Hsu (蘇昭旭): 台鐵 憶舊四十年,1945-1984 (*Taitie yijiu sishinian – 40 years of Taiwan railway memories, 1945-1984*), Taipei, 2000

Su Chao Hsu (蘇昭旭): 阿裡山森林鐵道, *Alishan Forestry Railway, 1912-1999,* Taipei 2001

Su Chao Hsu (蘇昭旭): 阿里山森林鐵路百年車輛史, *Rolling Stock of the Alishan Forest Railway through 100 years,* Taipei 2012

Su Chao Hsu (蘇昭旭)：台灣輕便鐵道小火車 – (*Taiwan qing bian teidao xiaohuoche – The Illustrated Handbook of Taiwan Light Railway and Industrial Railway Rolling Stock*), Xinbei, 2011

Su Chao Hsu: *A Brief History of Alishan Forest Railway Through the Century*, Chiayi, 2016

US Navy Department: *The Civil Affairs Handbook: Taiwan (Formosa) Taichu Province*, 1944

Wang Wenhao (汪文豪)：巍巍上谷關、戀戀久良栖—懷舊消失的八仙山森林鐵道, (*Wéiwéi shànggǔ guān, liàn liàn jiǔliáng qī— huáijiù xiāoshī de bā xiānshān sēnlín tiědào – Towering over the valley, loving Jiuliangqi – nostalgia for the Pahsienshan Forest railway*), in *Taiwan Forestry Journal*, vol 37, no1, 2011

Wei Zhi Hong (魏志宏)：八仙山林鐵歷史尋跡 (*Pahsienshan lintie lishixunji –* Tracing the history of the Pahsienshan Forest Railway) in 鐵道情報 (Rail News) no 134, 2002

Williams, Jack F: *Sugar: The Sweetener in Taiwan's Development* in Ronald G. Knapp ed.: *China's Island Frontier, Studies in the Historical Geography of Taiwan,* Honolulu, 1980

Wu Yong Hua (吳永華)：桃色之夢: 太平山百年自然發現史 – *Dream of peach: a century of discovery in the natural history of Taipingshan*, Yilan 2014

Xiao Jiufen (小九份)：林田山林場 (*Lintianshan Forestry Centre*), Taiwan 2009

Zhèng Rénchóng(鄭仁崇), Chén Fèngméi (陳鳳梅)，Chén Wénzhèng (陳文政): 林田山 史話 (*Líntiánshān history*), Taiwan 2009.

Unpublished material

Swift, Mike: private notes from a visit to the Pinghsi valley, November 1993

Zeng Shifang (曾世芳)：台糖五分車的建構與轉型文化產業經營之研究 – 以溪湖花卉文化園區觀光小火車為例 (The research of industrial operation for the Construction & Transformation culture of the sugar transport train of Taiwan Sugar Corporation). Master's dissertation, National Yunlin University of Science and Technology, Taiwan, 2006

Dulishan spiral, Alishan. Jhangnaoliao station in the valley below, seen from the third level of the spiral. The main line can be seen curving away to the left of the station as it descends towards Jhuci, the difference in grade between it and the lines in the station readily apparent.